Attaining The Mastership

Attaining The Mastership
Advanced Studies
On The Spiritual Path

Eliott James

Dhamma Books
Atlanta

Dedication

To Debbi, for her patience and support.

Contents

Attaining The Mastership

1

To Begin

In this book I attempt to write about the center life force within each of us, that being Soul. The thoughts that I express here are not part of a religion or philosophy, or even a metaphysical study, though these structures are a small part of the overall spiritual experience of Soul. In my experience the studies mentioned are but learning paths and stepping stones for us to reach into higher truths. We can develop the abilities of Soul in this life and uncover the real purpose of our being here.

Once Soul breaks free of the illusions, and It does this through knowledge, It lives in complete spiritual freedom with the fulfillment of *knowing* Itself and the worlds of GOD. The preceding words may say what other studies claim, and perhaps they have found this reality, too. But most studies claim to be the way, the path, the answer, yet can they show you the ability to *know* GOD, firsthand? Not a mental concept, not an emotional warmth, not a vague imagined image, but the actual experience of *being* in the presence of GOD?

There is a study that had been taught to only the few since time began in the Lower Worlds, and it concerns Soul and Its true purpose here. This study allows the individual to combine this unique information with personal experience to gain the knowledge that Soul is free of all limitations, if only

11

It realizes that. It teaches the base information of Soul awareness and how It can fully realize Itself and eventually, GOD ITSELF, while still within the physical body.

In recent years the basics of this knowledge was offered to a broad base of people, and many today study it. The information in this book is also part of that ancient teaching and deals with areas seldom brought out into the open before.

This knowledge can not be gained by reading books, but rather one must live and participate in the spiritual worlds. I was fortunate and blessed to have several inner Teachers who worked with me in the process, but they insisted I come to my own conclusions on what they showed me. You have to prove all of it to yourself each step of the way.

I remember sitting at my desk one evening and realizing that I never tried to walk a different path, in fact I once tried hard to be in step with everyone I knew. Many years ago it was important to me to be accepted within society's values. But, as long as I can remember, I wasn't satisfied in having what others had. I wanted to know what was behind the reasons, what made us who we are, why we are here, where we go and for what reason. It was always a struggle to try to belong and I felt compelled to take another route.

Eventually I realized that to survive I had to accept the ways of this life that could earn me a living. It was not others who were at odds with tradition, it was me. Whatever research I must do would be on my own time. Long after I was working knowingly with my Master it seemed I had to live in two different worlds for the most part, two different attitudes, two different personalities. One the world accepted and the other my private inner reality. It would have been easier to have gone along with everyone else's values, far easier. With time I concluded that I could not settle for less than what I wanted in my inner life. I had to listen to the voice within me, resisting only brought dissatisfaction and frustration. I could no longer settle for less. Two worlds began to blend into one. I found a oneness of attitude, though little appeared to change outwardly. Many years of change and challenge were to follow as I continued my personal search within.

Several years ago I lived alone in a small studio in an older part of Atlanta. The two rooms were simply furnished with a narrow desk and director's chair where I would write, a small bookcase, and a futon with quilt and pillow. Bamboo shades covered the windows and sliding door to the porch, and ficus trees contrasted the white walls and deep brown carpet.

I worked long hours at a job, and then as the summer sun fell behind the lush trees I would walk the old broken sidewalks of the neighborhood. I could see through the windows families eating dinner or the surreal moving light of a television in a darkened room. My world passed theirs in a matter of seconds. I would walk on and search my thoughts to clear the day and make contact again with the greater power I held within.

It was in those months of living in the studio that I made the most important decisions of my life, where I took the greatest risks and jumped from my own personal cliff into the worlds even deeper within. It was from that period on that I was able to speak completely in the first person from the knowledge of having experienced those realities firsthand.

This book has been in the writing for over fifteen years in one form or another, first as notes to myself. Along the way I thought I knew what lay ahead. I was mistaken. When I lived in the past, present or future I perceived many truths based on my understanding of what others said. Eventually I chose to live in only the moment, being aware of past and future, but not caught up in them. My viewpoint changed tremendously, and it is with this viewpoint that I abandoned all my past notes and notions and wrote this work from my realizations known *now,* not from the concepts or experiences of others. The single greatest point of any thing I may say should be that whatever we may believe to be true in our lives, whatever spiritual knowledge we hold, it has little value if it can not be lived actively every moment.

As I read over this manuscript I am reminded of many

other encounters with my Teacher, moments when I would sit in the darkness watching the moonlight filtered through the bamboo shade and I would hear His voice. Perhaps I should say that I sensed His voice, though at times a Master appears in a physical body. The inner reality is most often subtle, so much so that we usually allow our mind to override our sense of events within us. It has amused me to find that the outside world is the one of the greatest deception, the inner worlds are closer to our true selves. Of course, the inner and outer worlds interrelate, and we must see both to actually understand who and where we are.

One night in the studio I turned to a friend who had been my Master, and I asked, "How can I write about what you have shown me? Words seem so useless to describe the reality of what I realize."

He faced the bamboo shade and the soft rays reflected on His timeless expression.

"The teachings taught by the few honest and enlightened Masters all contain a Golden Thread of Truth, a sameness and single note of man's purpose.

"Though taught in different words and methods, in varying environments, spoken and written, uttered openly or scarcely hinted at, whether taught in the East or in the West, ten thousand years ago or in last night's dream, the Golden Thread of Truth has brought us along so that we may one day fully realize who we are.

"What you will write will be a representation of the Truth, the realization that you know. You cannot give someone else your understanding, you can only provide a catalyst for someone who is in the right place to receive it. You will always be alone in that only you know what you know, you can never fully share it with anyone else. Others may have the same basic understanding of the principle truth, but only you have your combination of experience and understanding that makes it yours."

He reached over and took a ficus leaf in His fingers, and then continued speaking.

"Words are made up of letters, which are symbols for sound. The vowel sounds of words are based on the eternal base of Sound, the letters symbolize the sound into written form. Symbols are born from the mental plane. When we write or speak we are transferring mental thoughts or images into a vocal or written form.

"Now, if your statement is based on concepts contained in the Lower Worlds then you will probably be able to find a way of communicating your thoughts. However, if you are trying to relate experiences or realizations from the Higher Worlds then you must first translate them into mental concepts, and then words. Much is lost in the translation, I'm afraid.

"Try to keep this in mind when working with people. You are drawing from resources inside of you that are made up largely from the Higher Worlds. It wasn't always like that, but you have developed the ability to work knowingly with this information. The mind does not want to accept what it cannot conceptualize, and the Higher Worlds are beyond the mind's ability to relate. The images you may find are but crude shadows to the brilliant truth. But that is the way that it is!

"All those given the task to teach others about the Higher Worlds have had this problem. Books have been written, and though the Teacher told them about this problem of translating, groups of people went about visualizing images of the Higher Worlds based on the dim accounts of His words. The followers eventually complained that they could not find the worlds described when they went within. They found other worlds, they felt different experiences were more significant. This is what was intended for them to do, but they had to discover it for themselves. Many had trouble exploring their personal world because they were looking for the worlds described in the Master's own words.

"Words are far from perfect when trying to relate your thoughts, when trying to share the Higher Worlds words are impossible. We use them because even in their shallowness words can sometimes be the catalyst to cause someone to look further into themselves. Remember, words are symbols for the eternal Sound, and even crude representations of the

Sound is better for Soul than no evidence of the Sound at all!''

Yes, I am reminded of many evenings spent listening to my Master, and also of many evenings when I would swear there wasn't another Soul to be found in all the worlds. The learning is in the living, the experience. This comes in many forms.

What I have written in this book is true. Perhaps you will want to prove all of it for yourself.

2
Enter:
This Life

I saw Him and knew there was only one decision I could make.

"You do not have to return," He said. But I did have to in order to gain what I had run away from before.

"You told me once that sometimes there are a million choices, yet there is only one we can make for that moment. This is that moment for me."

I felt His gaze and looked at Him. He smiled with a knowledge that bridged all the worlds of being and touched my heart with understanding.

"It is a good opportunity to fulfill your obligations. Remember, there is no hurry. Take your time if you like." He started to speak again but stopped.

"It will be the most difficult this time, won't it?" He did not answer me, He only smiled. I knew that every challenge I needed was possible in this next life, and I knew that I wanted what lay beyond the challenge. I had sensed it existed for centuries, but I had never dared to prove it for myself. Now the chance was here. I knew that all forces that be would stand in my way, but I also knew that it was the test that would make me complete.

I looked into the mist and saw the moment, I paused and glanced again at Him. He was silent in respect for my decision. I decided.

I awoke again in the second year, or so it had seemed like sleep, it was then but the conscious mind connecting with

Soul. I knew, but I was not sure of the conditions present. With one sense I realized the purpose, with the mind I doubted everything about me. But I had to persist. I would make it this time, I would.

The body developed an infection that took away my desire for food and caused my temperature to rage. My parents took me to the hospital, but the doctors were not aware of the full meaning of my condition. I was found hours later fevered at 107 degrees body heat. I slipped out of the dying shell and called out to Him, "What is happening?" I could only hear His voice.

"They are winning right now, they do not want you to make it this time. What do you want?"

"I do not want to be here," I replied.

"You don't have to be, you can find the experiences in another time."

I reflected on my decision to enter this world again and I knew I had to stay. I had prepared for lifetimes and had avoided the truth the last time around. I could not afford to run away again.

"This is not a test of time," He said. "You have as long as it takes, the decision is yours."

Again there was only one decision I could make. "I will stay. What do I do now?"

"You will fight and go on with your journey."

I gained consciousness screaming as they poured buckets of ice over me. The fever slowly left and they searched for veins large enough to pump new blood into that small, seemingly helpless body. The doctors hinted at the prospect of lifelong damage to the brain, and many prayed that I would continue to be the son that my parents wanted.

Years compounded on years and I knew only my life in that body, a childhood like many others, with my higher senses blocked from where I had been before and where I wanted to go.

Today I carry the scar from the cut-down on my ankle, and the experience deep within me, and knowledge that they did not win then. I did.

3

The
Old Man

When I was five or six years old my family lived in the Midwest, and every Summer my brother, sister and I would pile into the back seat of a red and white '57 Plymouth and travel through the Blue Ridge Mountains to see my grandfather. He had lived on a small farm in Carolina all of his life, and was largely a stranger to me. Even when my father was transferred back "home," and we visited Grandad every weekend, I did not really know him.

One hot day in the Summer we drove out to the country to see him, and while the family was discussing whatever families discuss, I was running in his eight foot high cornfield. I remember chasing one of his many dogs when I saw Grandad cross the row and follow a trail that led to the edge of the woods. I quietly walked behind him, trying to match his long stride by stepping in his tracks. The cornfield ended and the trail continued through rabbit grass and then into the trees. I could not see him but his tracks walked on.

I was afraid to go in the woods, but I was also lost in that part of the cornfield. I thought I heard someone talking, so I ventured into a thicket of hardwood. The air was cooler, and night had begun to fall first in the forest.

"Who are you?" someone seemed to call. I didn't dare say a word. Then there was absolute silence. My eyes began to search the limbs for an answer, and then darted from side to side. Perhaps it was time to move on, I reasoned. Just when I turned around to run as fast as I could, I ran into something big and I yelled at the top of my lungs.

He grabbed me up and looked me in the eyes. "Are you alright, boy?" he asked.

"There's something after me!" I cried, my feet still running with lightning speed.

"Slow down, boy. Nothing's gonna get you." Grandad set me on the ground and stooped down beside me.

"Just over that slope is an old owl, he's been in these woods for years. I remember one night, me and Harmon Griffen was comin' back from Jesse Geddings house, and we'd had a little bit to drink. Well, Harmon was mostly drunk, and we were walkin' up on these woods when we heard a low sound, it sounded like somebody, goin' 'humgh, humgh, humgh.' Harmon got scared, he said it was the devil. Well, I asked him how he knowed that, and he said that he'd heard him before, and we were in trouble if we stayed around there. About that time a bat flew right into the side of Harmon's head, knocked him down. I'd never seen one do that, and Harmon screamed for Jesus to save him right then and there, while he rolled over and over on the ground. I laughed, shah man, I was cryin' I laughed so hard!

"I tried to calm him down and told him it was just an owl in those woods, and a bat flew at him, that's all. But he wouldn't hear of it, and he got up and started runnin'. I saw him a couple of days later and asked him 'bout it. He said, 'hell man, I don't know what you mean, there ain't no devil, you know that.' I laughed and he got mad and walked off. People are funny."

Listening to his story, leaning against his knee and cradled in his big arms, this boy of seven discovered a long lost friend. It might have been his laughter, I don't know, but I did know that from that moment on we would be together.

Over the next four or five years I stayed with him off and on, just me and him in a simple concrete block house on a few acres in the country. He was in his seventies when I moved in, and farmed only a small plot with his mule and plow. He had never owned a car, so we traveled the twelve miles to

Pinewood in his wagon to buy supplies from the general store.

I was often with him in the winter, and we would gather at night in a middle room of the house, closing all adjoining doors to hold in the heat from a wood burning stove. He would tell many of the classic stories of his life, complete with the voices of the characters. Laughter filled the old house as I begged him to tell me about the time . . .

The coals would be dying in the late hours of the night when we would strip to long johns and pull back twenty pounds of quilts and hurry under them, the old springs of the iron bed crying out. I could look over and see his breath billowing in the cold dark, him still laughing as he remembered another time of his life. I realized that I was living in an era gone by, in his world, and I was more at home with him than anywhere else.

He was not one to go to church, as a matter of fact his whole family was after him to go most of his life, but he wouldn't. I saw him reading the Bible many times, and he would sing old gospel songs while playing the banjo. But church was inconsistent with his view of how one should live. He lived his religion in his every action, though I know he never thought of it that way. He just lived with a peace inside that came from appreciating his time here, and he gave of himself to almost everyone. He expressed laughter from deep inside because he knew pain was the alternative, and life was just too short to be unhappy.

Years passed and he sold the farm and moved in with my parents, sharing a room with my brother and me. It was almost as good as being in the country with him. He and I would sit in lawn chairs under the carport as the sun went down and watch children ride by on their bikes and bats circle the street lamps. An hour could go by without us saying a word, and yet we understood the time for what it was right then.

Years later, after I had moved away and would return to visit him, our family would still gather around the kitchen table until late in the night and listen to his stories, to his life and to his laughter. I have several hours of those late night sessions on tape, recorded at the time without his knowledge. Once he found out what I was doing, he insisted on me playing the tapes back for him to hear himself. That brought roars of laughter and prompted more stories on related topics. After each new story he would ask me, "Did you catch that?" And then we'd listen to the tapes all over again to more laughter.

At this point in my life I had begun to sense a deeper reality and was studying Eastern thought. It's funny, but for awhile I accepted the concept of reincarnation, and then I dismissed it as not being possible. It was on a visit home with him that I came to know that he and I had been together for so long, over many lives. I walked out to the carport and I saw him standing in the glow of the moon, and I *knew* our past all at once. It was that simple, yet incredibly profound. He knew it too but not in words or concepts. He knew it with an understanding that could not be expressed and accepted it as our bond together.

In being with him I saw life being lived instead of being analyzed and studied. I saw someone who felt comfortable giving but did not have to receive from others. I saw the human spirit alive, wanting nothing in a world where everyone was pursuing more. I saw him live his love of life and GOD, and I never heard him try to explain it.

4

Many
Years Ago

I had left the hot asphalt roads that criss-crossed the Eastern states, had enough of hitchhiking to every unknown college to play my restless songs. The glamourous life of a poet and completely unknown folk/rock songwriter had worn as thin as the elbows of my denim jacket. It was a big, heartless world I found out there, much different than the quiet of the Southern farmlands. But I had enough innocence to take me past most of the faces with no smiles, the cities without stars, and the hands outstretched for the duration. And as much as I gave of my innocence, I took back in experience, and then I decided to find the truth somewhere else.

I heard a part of the truth while standing at the top of a twenty foot ladder, reaching hard to put enough paint in a crack so as not to show from the ground. Stephen hired me as his second man and taught me the painter's trade. He threw in a good dose of Eastern mysticism at no extra charge. It was my first real exposure to the Bhagavad Gita and to someone who attempted to live life from that viewpoint. We would talk for hours, me mostly listening, as we spent the best part of a summer painting old houses various shades of yellow and blue.

One of my fondest memories is hearing one version of a balanced man: "He that is in tune with all things can dive into a pond and not make a ripple, not make a sound." I've never met anyone who could do that, but I love the vision that it creates.

I went on to read many interpretations of the passages from the Bhagavad Gita and the Upanishads. As new as it was, it was also familiar, and at the time I could not explain that. These works deal with reincarnation among other things. They are written from the mystic attitude, not so much in plain view, and I had no concrete proof of whether I had other lives or not. But the ideas were not entirely foreign. The names were, however. To this day I dislike having to learn a new name and pronunciation for something that exists quite nicely in English.

About this time I heard a heated discussion on talk radio about astral projection. A woman who sounded very educated was explaining to the talk show host how people could separate a part of themselves when they slept and travel to any point on the planet while their body snoozed undisturbed. I loved it. Here was a woman on the radio who had every Southern Baptist in Atlanta calling to announce her future in hell. I had read where mystics had been said to have projected hundreds of years ago, but here was a woman living in that very city who did it the night before. I wanted to get to the bottom of that so I drove right over to the radio station and waited. Soon a proper-looking lady in her fifties emerged and we proceeded to talk about roving spiritual bodies late into the night.

Though I don't read many books these days I used to read a lot, and I must have read two dozen books on astral projection. I would do that on every philosophical and metaphysical subject I uncovered. All the books said something different, and yet they all sounded the same. Again there was something familiar about this, but all my efforts to leave my body by astral projection failed.

I threw up my hands one night and decided to just meditate. I had a small apartment and had hung an Indian print bedspread from the ceiling to create a veiled corner in the living room. In the draped area I had a small carved wooden table and a brass incense burner in the shape of a snake. That night I put on a record of sitar and flute, lit a cone of incense, and breathed deeply while lying on the floor. When I awoke the room was dim, the record was stuck in the last grooves, and the incense black. And someone was standing in the room. I couldn't see him, or it, but I knew someone was standing right in front of me. Every sense I had was tingling with anticipation. I was terrified. What was this power that could be in front of me but not be seen?

After an eternity it dawned on me that anything that powerful could do away with me if it wanted, and it hadn't yet, so there was no point in being scared. There wasn't a lot I could do about it anyway, so I gave up! I sat there suddenly calm and then became curious. What was this? I stood up and walked to the other side of the room. The energy remained in the one spot, and I could feel it looking at me. I walked very slowly up to where it was, saying nothing. I did not feel evil coming from it, just a warm power that radiated slowly from it and then back to it, much like the waves near the shore. I seemed to be in its aura of outgoing and incoming energy. I reached out my hand and felt a burning sensation in my palm, a tickling current taking up the invisible space of this being. I stood there for a long while. Finally I sat down on the sofa across the room and I sensed the energy fading. I could not think, I could only know that I was part of something much greater than me for a few moments, and then I was back in a lifeless room of shadows.

It was that night that a true connection was made between me and the greater reality. I did not know what it all meant, I had no idea where I was going, but soon I discovered that the energy in my living room that night was the inner form of my Teacher. I wasn't able to see with my inner sight then, so He manifested His energy in that way so that I would respond to the opportunity.

Astral projection and the Bhagavad Gita become far less important as He began to work with me. I would speak with Him in dreams, though for a long time I never looked directly at Him. My Teacher was always standing at my left hand side, we would view a scene together, and we would speak without seeming to talk.

This scared me from time to time, and I wondered if I was losing my mind. I wasn't able to astral project, or if I did I didn't know it, but there was someone very powerful and wise who talked to me in my dreams. As much as I wanted an experience in my life I wasn't at all sure that I wanted the one I was having. These experiences weren't ones I could touch or even talk about with Stephen. What my Teacher told me seemed real and, again, familiar, but why was He telling me these things?

There was always a choice, He said. I could turn my back on much of it and live like everyone else. It was my decision. What was the reward of the changes, where was it all leading to? I had a thousand questions that weren't being answered. He said it was step by step, one thing at a time, and in looking back I know that He didn't lie. That's just the way it's been, and really the only way it can be. It's when we look back over the single experiences that we collect them into a past time frame and make a life map of our journey.

5

The
Next Step

There are dozens of publicized aspects of the spiritual path. There are the subjects in metaphysics, the countless variations of Eastern and Western religions, and philosophies. I've put the metaphysical, philosophical and religious aspects together because while they are different, they are in fact equal in their value. They are all learning experiences for Soul.

Where does one begin the personal search? You can only begin where you are. You will start with the information closest to you and then step logically to other areas. The material will build on itself; one aspect will suggest others that interrelate with it. This is true because it is impossible to truly separate one from the other, they are all part of the whole picture. We can seemingly isolate a subject and elaborate to great degree about it, but we have but focused for a time on a small part of the big picture. Knowing this is helpful when we begin our search for truth, because it may help to keep us from becoming too deeply involved with one area and lose sight of our goal.

What is the goal? It would be easy for me to tell you what my goal was and is today, but your goal is reserved for you to decide. Your goal is the only one that is important. The goals will change as you grow further into the truth that you discover.

And what is truth? Truth is simply what you believe to be true for you, nothing more or less. There are set laws that govern the many worlds of GOD, and there are relative laws that govern single worlds of GOD. You are subject to the action and reaction of these laws whether you know of them or not, so that's a strong case for finding out about them. But truth is a subjective reality for you. If you do not know about something at all, then it does not exist for you. When you hear about a subject you will likely put it in one of three categories: true, untrue, or not yet known; these conclusions being based on your experience. This is part of the personal examination process that we all go through to find our value of truth. Life is subjective, there is no objective truth except in the mental concept that when two or more people agree on a point it is a reality, therefore an objective conclusion. In my experience, if someone has to agree with me for me to believe what I know myself then perhaps I never knew it to begin with!

After beginning to have dreams with my Teacher, I tried to adopt a life of meditation, an attitude of devotion. This seemed like the correct attitude to take, though He never instructed me to feel that way. I can't say I was unsuccessful but it is difficult to undo twenty years of Western training in several months. I was trying to become more spiritual by changing my habits and attitude, not realizing then that these changes come from the inside out. All the righteous living and devotion in the world will not get us closer to GOD, but when we advance on the spiritual path inwardly it is normal that our outer life is changed too.

I was somewhat of a dreamer and poet then and not yet giving sixty hours a week to a career. The simple lines of ancient Japanese poetry perhaps best represented the peace that I wanted for myself. But life was not as simple as the ancient poetry, except for isolated moments. Life was quite complex and full of contradictory forces. I had made contact with a force so much greater than myself and I thirsted for more. I wanted to be an active part of whatever it was, and I knew I was a long way from knowing just what it was. As afraid as I was of part of this mystery, it was indeed a mystery and I had to know more.

The first dreams with my Teacher consisted mostly of me sensing Him beside me, and sometimes I would remember walking through a forest filled with vivid colors. Often I would wake up not remembering any details, but I would feel that I knew something I didn't know before.

About four months after my experience in the living room, I reluctantly went to bed late one night. My mind was full with the sounds of the summer forest through the open window, yet I was aloof and not involved as I closed my eyes. A moment passed and I was standing beside someone who was a friend, though I did not think to look at Him and I really did not know who He was. Talking with Him seemed like the most natural thing I could do, and it seemed that we had been together for lifetimes.

"I don't know what to do." I said, though there really were no words spoken.

"What do you want in your life?" He asked.

"I want to know, I want to be able to know what this is about. Where am I going, what's the purpose?"

"The purpose is to find GOD, that is the direction of the journey. To do this you simply have to be yourself."

I didn't understand at all. "Can we know GOD?" I asked.

"You can be a knowing part of the greatest force that IS, you can see part of the Creator ITSELF. Some people call this GOD."

"What happens then?"

"To do this you will explore many paths, you will abandon them, you will take the lessons to your heart one by one. You will face the call of your own needs, then surrender to the needs of the whole. You will do this when there is no other joy that exists except the joy of being an active part of IT. Then you may *know* a part of IT. And you may decide your own path from there."

"Do we become one with GOD, an atom in the Creation?"

There was a moment of silence and then He said, "If you

want to do that you can. Some Souls spend considerable periods basking in the radiance of the SUPREME. You'll probably get bored with it, however. You can also work with the will of GOD in any of the many worlds of IT. You decide."

"Where do I begin? I've tried to project my astral body, and I meditate. What do I do?"

"There are many, many areas to examine. They are almost worthless until you learn one of the most important laws of all the worlds. You are responsible for your own actions."

I waited. "Is that it?" I asked.

"Everyone wants to control the phenomenal works, they want to read minds, spin their bodies through space, and heal the multitudes. This is not the meaning of life, these can be some of the more obvious effects of the searching Soul. Appearances are deceiving, more in the material realm than the inner reality. Instead of being interested in performing occult skills we should first be concerned about our own place in the play of life.

"Know this. No one makes you do anything without your agreeing to it. No exceptions. For every action there is a reaction. You get what you give. No one else is responsible for your mistakes or your triumphs. You are all you have in the end result. Think about this, it will change your life.

"When you are aware of the intent of your every thought, feeling and action then you will be in control of your life. You will decide what you will do. You will find the answers right before you as you need them, you will pay the prices for the experience. Willingly.

"When you control your own life and allow everyone the freedom of their own world, then you will see yourself in a new reality, a new awareness. This is not for the mind to believe, this is for you to *know* with every bit of your being, and to live it! Not many people realize the importance of this.

"Responsibility and knowingness are the twin forces you have for your personal power. These are the causes, the endless aspects of cults and studies are the effects. You must always be the cause or the willing effect. You must know the laws and their actions."

"Will you teach me how to do this?"

"I can teach you nothing, you must find this for yourself. Think about it, begin your journey with those thoughts."

I opened my eyes while sitting up at the head of my bed. I was captured in a profound silence. It was at least half an hour later when I realized that I had been dreaming. And then I wondered how a dream could be so real.

I had only to look at my own personal life to learn some of the lessons of responsibility. Most of the problems we face in this area are from the innocent ideas and character molds we are exposed to as children. I say innocent because rarely do people know of the spiritual law concerning personal responsibility. We tend to accept behavior around us if it is supported by most other people.

The spiritual law on responsibility is really very simple and basic. We are accountable for every action of thought and deed. We receive what we give, and each of us must give the other person their personal freedom to live their own life as they see fit. Each of us must knowingly use our own personal freedom for the experiences we need to grow by in this world. So why is this so hard to live in practice?

Affairs of the heart entangle us in other people's lives to a point that we may not know where our feelings begin and the other person's end. Often there is a warming bond between us, but there can also be misunderstanding and pain. So often we feel that someone put us into a situation that we had no control over, or we feel that we were hurt by someone's actions because we love them and have no choice.

As we interrelate with people, be it in the home, at work, or in the world at large, we are constantly pulled into someone's desires or space. And if we are willing to participate, then that presents no problem. But often we feel like there is no choice, that we had to be a part of someone else's actions. But we do not.

Each one of us stands alone and complete within ourselves. No one has the right to enter our private world or space without our permission, and so naturally we do not have the right to enter their world without theirs.

We find that we must take responsibility for our actions, that no one caused us to do anything that we ourselves did not allow to happen. Thus, if we desire personal freedom in our own lives then we must give that freedom to everyone else. We must develop the ability to respond to other people's actions while maintaining control, so that we can be the cause, not the effect. If we should choose to participate we may become willing effect, but this is done with our full knowledge and permission.

When we feel that we are forced to react instead of willingly acting we lose the personal freedom that we truly possess. For example, anger is largely seen as being under someone else's advantage, a response in answer to an unfair action taken by another. But by being angry we are responding to something that is not our business, and we are being affected by a force outside our own. What I'm trying to say here is that it doesn't matter what others do, think or say, we must give them the freedom to be themselves, as long as it does not affect us directly. When they interfere directly in our personal space then we have the right to act, but not because someone is or thinks a certain way. One of my favorite expressions is, "It's none of my business what you think about me!"

So much confusion comes when we desire to have a measure of control over others, when we want something to happen our way, and when it is something that concerns more than just ourselves. But we do not have the right to take what is not ours, and the viewpoint of others is not a matter of control, it is simply their own expression. It is enough that we take care of our own environment and lives; which does not depend on the concern, support, or influence of others; unless we should desire and allow it.

So really there is no one to blame for our troubles but ourselves. There is no one who can change our lives but ourselves. There are no exceptions.

Many in the world are concerned with collective society, the wrongs inflicted upon a group, the responsibilities of those in power to take care of all the rest. This thinking has never worked for long in all the history of mankind. It has always been the individual who has the choice of running his own life or allowing others to take control of his life. Most people are not aware that they alone can make that personal decision of freedom.

Spiritual freedom is within. Spiritual responsibility interlaces with that freedom, which affects every aspect of our lives.

6
To
Know GOD

Before you *know* GOD you will realize that each moment is the only reality you have control over, the past being gone and the future not yet here. By living each moment to the fullest you are not only far happier with what you have, you are also living in one of the highest spiritual principles. This is the principle that you have only to be who you are, right now, and you will see through the illusions that have been structured around you. By practicing this you are able to better use your abilities to gain knowledge in the other worlds. This knowledge offers the understanding that all roads lead to home for you, as Soul.

The knowledge and power that comes with experience is the understanding of GOD's worlds and the power to step out of the illusions about you. You do not have to wait to find heaven, and you can *know* GOD, *here* and *now.* You have only to be all that you can *be,* and with time you will find IT to be THE REALITY. You do not find GOD through drugs or extensive ordeals of trance, but by simply *knowing* the truth of your existance.

I was brought up with Christian beliefs, and once I seriously considered the ministry. Matters that were spiritual always concerned me, even as a child. There was a natural curiosity for the why's of our life here, and I've always known there was a Creator who put this play in motion. The explanations of the church rarely satisfied me however, and from time to time I sought answers from the world.

As a teenager I was rather rebellious for a period and wanted to leave the public schools, but I was underage. A small Catholic school gave me shelter from the state requirements and allowed me to study completely on my own. I chose theology and poetry. To me they were companion subjects, one as man's spiritual struggle to understand, the other as the finest expression of that limited understanding.

I never seemed to fit into organized religions, because they are by their nature designed to apply to a broad base of people who will follow them. After all I've studied, the groups I've joined, the services I've attended, they were but interesting and educational investigations. I've followed my own way, which has led to a fair amount of misunderstanding for my family and friends. But there is a common thread that runs through all beliefs concerning a Creator and our place in the Creation. Few people realize this directly for themselves, choosing instead to accept the thoughts and convictions of others as their decisions on their place in the worlds of GOD.

It had been two years since my last dream experience with the Teacher. I had been studying the methods we worship GOD by, the reasoning, and the history. But what about GOD ITSELF and me? What is GOD and what am I? All of the writings allude to it, but do not address it directly. Why?

The Golden Thread that runs through all studies is, in fact, knowing that there is a very personal bond between GOD and Soul. The writers of truly inspired works know this. This can be stated and talked about, but it is really beyond any words or concepts we may find. At some point on the spiritual path each of us will come to know this deep within. My Teacher told me earlier that the purpose of life was to know GOD. This seemed to be a mystical reference but not a reality to me. But it is that simple.

GOD is at one end of the Golden Thread, and each of us is at the other end. We follow it until we know GOD. That became my goal, it burned inside of me and I knew that all would pass away and I would continue until reaching my goal. That was a profound moment for me. I did not then know of the many worlds of creation, the challenges ahead, the steps I would take that would explain so many of my questions. I only had a deep sense of recognition within me that I was on my way to finding the truth.

One night I was taking a late walk through the quiet suburban streets of North Atlanta. The October wind stirred leaves and the tops of trees around me. I stopped under a giant oak and sat down, leaning back against it. I do not remember closing my eyes.

"Do you know what you want?"

"I want GOD," I replied to my Teacher sitting next to me.

"What of responsibility? Have you forgotten?"

"I have searched my life and I am now responsible."

"Yes, you are in many ways. It is the subtle ways we must see. In every action we must draw our lines of participation, giving each one the freedom of their own actions, the burden of their own proof. You must let go of people. You must find your own way, you owe them little."

"Can we really know GOD?" He did not answer. "What is He like?" I asked.

"There are many worlds of creation, there are many beings believed by faiths to be GOD. A few people have met beings so powerful in such strange worlds that they thought it was indeed GOD in His heaven, while they were in trance or dream, and went on to write their experiences and create religions. But rarely has this been GOD. You must walk through these worlds yourself and find IT."

"What will I find?"

"You will find the experiences that will complete you as Soul, you will recognize the differences between the perceived experience and IT of ITSELF."

"What is IT?"

"IT. GOD. There are thousands of names for the Creator, every group of man has a word for IT. Of course there can be no word that describes that magnificent energy that has brought all this together. You must experience this for yourself to understand, then you will smile and simply *know* the reality while using some name to describe IT.''

"Is there one way to IT?"

"Yes, there is but your way for you. For every Soul there is one individual path to GOD, each a slightly different way and pace. You will find yours."

"Where should I begin?"

"Begin where you are."

"There are hundreds of ways," I said in confusion.

"They all are aspects of GOD. In each study you will find principles that apply to that world of action you are in and some that are eternal principles. That is the reason for studying them, to find the lessons within them. You need not study them all, however. There are so many different studies because there are so many splintered paths to GOD. There are a limited number of principles for you to know. Two people undergoing the same study will likely walk away with different benefits of the study. The worth is not in the study itself but what you gain from it.

"Each study will take you only so far, you will know when to go on. Some say the Wheel of Life can average eighty-four thousand lives. If you attempt to master each aspect, you will think you will never reach GOD. See the truth wherever you are, then journey on.

"If you think of knowing GOD, then you are setting up the image that your life will fulfill; and if you fill this image with desire, you will find the goal sooner. But there is one point you should realize. If you find GOD through your mind and emotions, you will find an astral and mental manifestation of GOD and you will live with the emotions and mind satisfied with the discovery. This is not GOD.

"If in your life you are filled with the desire for GOD then you will not find GOD, as you must be free of all desire. When you first desire GOD you will seek IT, the desire being the focus of your energy. When you do not find IT you will discover your true need for IT, or you will abandon your search. If your need is great to find IT, you will because you no longer desire."

My mind whirled with the information He was giving me. "What is GOD if I can't realize IT?"

"The so-called God realizations of these Lower Worlds are dim aspects of GOD, they are very limited manifestations of GOD. In truth, they are Soul and must move within the life realization cycle as all Souls do. You can realize these and grow by them but there is more beyond these worlds. In the areas of Higher awareness one does not realize God, one *knows* GOD by *being* in the presence of IT, ITSELF. The mind has nothing to do with this knowledge; the emotions are not part of this discovery. Soul is aware of GOD without the hinderance of the lower bodies. This is *knowing.* "

"Sometimes I feel so alone, there is no one to talk to about what's happening to me."

"When you are discouraged remember that you have made the inner connection with a Teacher. For so long we work toward that time, and once we establish that connection we are close indeed to finding our way. Everyone needs someone to guide them through the unspeakable darkness that exists. You can go far without a guide, but you cannot find your goal without the help of someone who has been there before you. One day you will be totally on your own, there is really no other way it can be. You are!"

"Will you always be my Teacher?"

"I've watched you for a long time, and then you asked for guidance."

"Was that you in my living room?"

There was silence. The affection I felt for Him overwhelmed me.

"You will have many Masters to guide you. Each will show you a special task. Soon you will find a study founded by one of these Masters. By reading His books and working with Him directly on the inner planes you will grow very rapidly.

"The best way is to work with a Teacher on the inner worlds and in person. This way was possible for the few over the past thousands of years. We must now step up the pace of spiritual unfoldment. To reach more who are ready, one man has written down information that was never before readily available. He spoke to groups openly and made known His position. A very rare event for this world. His work is now studied by many on this planet.''

"Will He teach me how to find GOD?" I asked.

"Why don't you ask Him?"

The dawn was held behind the tangled branches of the motionless trees. I must have walked home but I don't remember it. The air around me was alive and I felt a burning inside of me that cried to be answered. I wanted to know more!

7

The
Passing

I had read so many books, and I had joined a few study groups, but really I held only a head full of information. My heart still sensed the presence of my Master, even though it had been many, many months since making contact with Him.

I had been working with retarded children, and then I worked with the elderly at a local hospital. I had married and started a family, and our first child was only a few days from being born. I was sleeping restlessly, and the dreams I was having! They were clouded at the time, the details vague, but when I looked into the eyes of my infant daughter a few days later I knew that the dreams had something to do with her. It was only years later, when I had the ability and the awareness to recapture that time, that I found that I had been in contact with her in the dream state before she was born into this world. We had discussed the difficult changes likely for us to go through, and I assured her of my support through those times. She decided to be born in this time and place.

A couple of weeks after her birth I was standing in the checkout line of a discount store when a paperback book reached out and grabbed me from the rack. It is entitled, *Life After Life,* by Raymond Moody, and deals with case histories of people who had "died" and come back, much to the surprise of the doctors involved. It describes scenes of dying and the peaceful transition, as well as accounts of the afterlife they experienced. The book is written in a simple and straightforward manner, much different than the mystical books I was used to reading. At the time I found it very interesting, and filed the information away in my internal storage of data. Life was full and moving with a new child in my life.

It was three o'clock or so on one cloudy day in November, and I had just finished making my rounds on the third floor of the hospital, providing physical therapy to elderly patients in their rooms. I entered the staff elevator and as the doors closed I felt almost dizzy and seemed to step out of myself. I was then aware of being at the side of my grandfather, he was lying in a hospital bed, pale and thinner than when I last saw him. He looked at me, reached for my arm, and gasped for air as he died.

I became aware of the elevator doors opening and nurses coming in. I leaned back against the stainless steel walls and gathered myself. For half an hour afterwards I walked the halls trying to analyze what I thought might have happened, but I wasn't at all sure it could be based on anything but imagination.

I heard my name being paged over the speakers. A call was waiting from my mother. She didn't know how to tell me, but the local hospital had just called to tell her that my grandfather had died suddenly. She apologized for not telling me he had been admitted a few days before, as no one believed it to be serious. His heart had failed and she said he had died alone but I knew that he hadn't. I was with him.

A thousand thoughts raced through me, with a sadness I had not felt before in this life. After the initial shock of his passing, as I was driving back from his funeral, I realized how the book at the checkout stand had helped me to better accept his death. Death was no longer an abstract premise, it was real and immediate in my being. I was somewhat comforted in knowing that throughout the world other people were confirming what my inner Teacher had told me. There is continuous life. Death is only for an instant. But those of us who remain in this physical world still feel the loss and sadness of the passing of one we love.

That night I drove to the country home where I first met him. I parked beside the "old house," the wooden frame home where he had lived for forty years. Looking across the grove of pecan trees veiled in soft moonlight I remembered his laughter. I followed the sandy two-fingered road that bordered the cornfield and weaved in and out of overhanging trees. There in the thick brush was the giant rock he and two other men, with a mule, pulled out of the field in 1953. He saw it fall from heaven afire and watched it for days before attempting to move it from its crater. When I was a boy he showed it to me with an air of mystery in his voice. The rust colored hunk of iron still sat beside the road, pocked from the heat of its journey to Earth.

The memory still rich in my mind, I paused and recalled another night with him. We were walking this old road when I asked him where the sliver of moon that hung in the eastern sky came from. He told me that God trimmed his thumb nail and set it in the heavens for man to be reminded of Him. Yes, I was reminded of Him, and then a deep sense of loss swept over me and I wondered where Grandad was. I looked into the heavens and saw clouds backlighted with the fullness of the moon and I wanted more than anything to talk with Grandad again.

As I walked on the sorrow lifted, at first I was not aware of it, but then I found myself laughing silently. We used to do that, walking down this road, we would just laugh to ourselves with no spoken reason. Out of the corner of my eye I caught a glimpse of someone, and I turned to my left suddenly. It was Grandad, though a faint image, it was him! We just looked at each other and he smiled. After a few minutes the intensity overwhelmed me and I closed my eyes. When I opened them he was gone, though I could still hear his laughter.

The next day I started to drive back to Atlanta when I decided to visit his grave one last time. It was not a big cemetery and I had known several people who were buried there when I was growing up in that small town. I turned in to the narrow entrance and followed the one lane road to the new section of graves. I got out of the car and expected to see the fresh dirt and flowers, but his grave wasn't there. I walked for hundreds of yards in all directions but could not find the spot. Frustrated, I got in the car and left the cemetery, then drove back and attempted to find the site again. His grave wasn't there. I sat on the hood of the car and wondered what was going on. Sitting there for twenty minutes I eventually relaxed while watching birds search the fresh mowed grass. I sensed a voice deep inside me saying, "He is not here, you met with him last night. He is always with you in your heart."

I left the cemetery and that small town, and I have never been back to stand at his grave. He's not there.

Death was a mystery until later I read of what happens in the dying process. Still it was not real to me, and I had to go on to prove the experience for myself. This came several years later and involved a study of leaving the body awareness willingly and exploring other realms. We do not actually leave the body, rather we shift our awareness to another point of experience within us. When we shift our awareness this can normally last for an hour but not much more, and we can view and take part in another plane of action. We then return our awareness to the physical body which was asleep or in contemplation.

In the dying process the bond Soul has with the body is broken and awareness is only blocked for an instant with some people. Some studies mention a silver cord that connects Soul to the various bodies, and this is basically true. When we shift awareness the cord remains intact, but in physical death the cord is severed. The person then becomes aware of being in a new environment, an interim place where a smooth transition can take place. Sometimes we are greeted by friends and relatives but not always. There are beings responsible for this transition, and a Master oversees the process. For the Soul who knowingly worked with a Master while alive, He is there to escort Soul. If there were physical injuries that caused a violent death, then there were likely emotional reactions that must be balanced, and this is taken care of at that time.

The time spent in this interim awareness varies by the need of the individual, and time is also marked differently in this area of the astral plane, but generally one is not there very long. There is a review of the karmic implications involved, and the beings that work in this area assist in determining where the Soul would be best suited to continue on the learning cycle. This is the judgment so often referred to in religious writings, and Soul is aware of this review and of the actions and reactions It participated in while inhabiting a physical body.

Karma is the balancing of actions, whether we know of them or not, and the beings in the interim awareness help to find the environment that will help Soul balance the karmic debt involved. The balancing is exact in both debt and payment, and can seem cold and sometimes cruel to one who does not understand the bigger picture.

It may be that the needs are best served by Soul entering another area of the astral plane, or any one of the Lower World planes. One interesting note is that experiences are greatly accelerated in the material world, on this planet, and it is somewhat difficult to be reborn here. There are many wanting to take care of their obligations, and it will generally take less time in the material world. So there's a line, if you will.

If you have followed a Master while living here you will be dealt with directly by Him and He will determine the best course for you to follow. For those more advanced on the spiritual path, there are choices and decisions that can be made by the individual as to the life Soul will follow next.

If there is a hell to be known it is perhaps when Soul is made aware of the karmic responsibilities involved and when realizing the result of Soul's actions in the past life and the need to balance this load. It can seem sad at the time but this is the way Soul learns and grows. There is no fire and brimstone that Soul will have to endure, except in the perceptions created by the minds of men. There are places in the lower astral world that resemble man's descriptions of hell, and Souls are there but not as punishment as such, it's just their needed experience. There are places on this planet that I have seen that are indeed hell, but people were living there by their choice. Perhaps in their awareness they did not see it as being hell. Perhaps they did and chose not to change their lives. It is much the same in the other worlds.

If Soul has balanced the karmic debts then It does not have to return to the physical worlds for rebirth. It can dwell in the area of Its awareness, which may be the mental plane. If Soul awareness was fully gained then It will return there and never again have to endure the cycle of rebirth. From there It will continue to gain realization of the Higher Worlds but does not undergo a dying process.

If Soul is greatly attached emotionally to the life it is being forced to give up by dying it may linger between the physical world and the interim awareness. This normally will pass as Soul realizes that It no longer has a material body and must move on. Sometimes there is unfinished business that Soul feels must be resolved before It can peacefully transfer.

From time to time Soul is stubborn and will stay attached to the life It wanted by playing on the emotions and energy of someone It knew while in the body, or It can remain here by sheer will based in anger. It may take someone with the ability to show this Soul what is really happening to cause Soul to transcend. We can easily sense Soul's presence when It is caught between these worlds and often can see with our astral sight a faint image of the astral body.

My wife and I bought a house that had two Souls staying in one end of it. At first their presence did not bother me, but increasingly they were upsetting the household. By researching the situation I discovered that there had been a terrible fire in a house in the 1930s that stood partially where our house stands now. A young boy and his older teenage sister died largely because the father was drunk one night and carelessly set the wood frame house afire. They died struggling to get out of the flames. They both were bitter and would strike out often because they were so out of balance by being between this world and the astral plane. Their hate for their father, who they never had a good relationship with, and their bitterness from not being able to participate in the life they wanted, held them to this spot.

Communicating with them didn't work, in fact, it angered them more. Their presence didn't bother me in itself, and I respected their desire to be where they were. One night they upset my wife by surrounding her and invading her emotional body with fears and suspicion, and they attacked me as well. Enough was enough so I used personal energy to change the vibratory environment of where they stayed, forcing them to transcend into the astral. They have not returned, and in fact, cannot return.

Those who work with a Master and have developed the ability to shift their awareness easily will hardly miss a beat when shedding their physical body. There will be little fear, if any, and they will be in the presence of a Master who will guide them to where they need to be. Death is a subtle transition, much more subtle than we would believe. It is the fear of the unknown that hurts most of us and holds us back from experiencing something new. Those who take up the active spiritual path are taught slowly to break their attachments to this world and to be bold in the search for themselves. "Only the brave know GOD," my Master has told me. He was right.

It is natural to feel an emotional sorrow and loss when someone close to us dies. The mind is set in patterns and will hesitate to accept not having the familiar images around that it knows. Deep in our hearts, our Soul awareness, we may know that our loved one has simply shifted awareness while their physical body drops away. Perhaps this can be a small comfort until the mind and emotions come into balance.

Seeing my grandfather that night on the road was the bond that we had holding him to this world until he communicated his love again to me. Fulfilling that, he passed to the interim plane. My affection for him was tremendous and for a long time in my youth I had him on a pedestal. This only increased with his death.

One night, several years later, I was with him in the dream state by shifting my awareness to where he was then, residing on the astral plane. We were riding in the back seat of a car in the countryside where we had lived. I became excited and reminded him of the many stories he used to tell me, and how we could spend time together now just like it was before. He looked at me sternly and said that I was living in the past memories of my childhood, and that he had many faults that he had to deal with. The car stopped and when I got out I woke up screaming, "No." He was trying to help me to let go of the perfect memories and to see him for who he had truly been, a man with great strengths but with many weaknesses. One evening shortly after that experience I met him again.

Inner Reunion

Hovering by the broken frame on the wall
is your image as I know it was,
though you stepped aside
three years ago this Fall.
You stand quietly, head slightly down
before the aged photograph
placed behind dulled glass.

I've wished to see you many times
and looked for you
in every field I passed while driving.
I've asked where you were
when the world grew deaf and sullen.

Finally I let go
and chose to laugh with you again,
but in honored silence.

With my pen thumping
the binding of this book of scribbled poems,
not thinking of you at all,
well there you are
on the vivid screen of my mind,
more real than I thought could be.
My eyes swell with tears.
You, an unseparable friend,
showing me how to know you again.

Though Earth's forms decay and stand broken,
all the force of life
revolves within the sphere of inner sense.

Dear friend, no words were really needed then,
none are really needed any more.

He had been dead six years when a friend I worked with was killed in a car crash. I went home that evening and was sad in losing my friend, but not really very upset. I felt quiet most of the night until looking out the window. I started to laugh and then a flood of tears poured from deep within me. Losing the friend brought up the locked away emotions of losing my grandfather. I cried for hours, and woke up crying the next day. At last I had let go of my emotional attachment to what we had when we were together here. I was then freed from that hold of the past.

We meet from time to time now. I go to where he is which is much the same as it always was. He hates to travel. He's doing well and still laughs with a fullness of being very happy with his life. We will be friends forever.

8
How We Come to Know

Two years passed since Grandad died. I was devoting a great deal of time to a new career of selling wholesale automotive products. It was an outwardly challenging time for me. I had started a family and was attempting to build a comfortable lifestyle and to study the spiritual works as I could. The fire still burned inside but was a smaller flame. I had no clear path to follow at that time, so I quietly pondered the mysteries whenever I could.

I would take late night walks from time to time and often stop and look into the heavens. What was I here to do on this planet? I could honestly say that very little held my interest for long, not the business and not the occult books. There was no one to talk to about what I felt. Life was comfortable but not happy.

One of my accounts was a heavy-duty truck repair facility which I called on weekly. The buyer's name was Hutch, a friendly fellow in his late thirties. His tight shirts emphasized his solid build, as he would stand before me smiling, head slightly down, a cigarette dangling from his lips. He rolled his short sleeves up further and usually had a pack of cigarettes tucked away there. We were a sight side by side. I wore my hair long, as was the style then, and he wore his very short.

We didn't talk much at first. We'd exchange opinions about the weather or something and then I'd make my selling

pitch. He'd politely listen and then begin to explain the needs
of the company. Very nicely to let me know that there was
very little I could offer them, just the nickel and dime odds
and ends. I was happy with that for the time.

One chilly morning I called on him early. A heavy frost
blanketed the grass outside the door. We greeted each other
and started to comment on the weather when he began telling
me of a theory that could greatly change the patterns of
weather as we knew it. He went on for fifteen minutes, expanding from the weather to the forces that controlled the
Earth itself. I was fascinated. I asked him where he got this
information but he would say very little about the source of
his knowledge. Over the following weeks we discussed more
of his ideas and I persisted in wanting to know where they
came from.

One day he handed me a book as I greeted him. He said it
was the foundation of his beliefs, he was studying a series of
discourses written by this same man. I thanked him and
when I went back to my car I thumbed through the pages of
the book. Six hours later he surprised me by knocking on the
windshield. I had read most of the book and hadn't realized
the time!

That book was one of the greatest influences of my life,
and it ranks with two others written by the same author.
They are easily the greatest books on the planet today. I knew
instinctively every word I read, as if I had heard it all before.
I had found the path and the writings by the Master that my
Teacher told me of. I sent away for the discourses and began
a four year association with the outer organization. Today I
still drop in on a class now and then and keep up with some
of the people I met, but I am not now a member of any
organized group. I know that this work is the highest study
possible in the outer world, and I support their efforts in
making this information available.

As a footnote I'll add that my buyer friend, and we are
still close friends, later left the outer teaching he introduced
me to. There is a time for all things and then a time to
change. This is the natural flow of all nature.

A major part of that study was a series of exercises that

would allow me to shift awareness to greater realms of knowledge. The purpose of this is to gain information and experience that is not as readily available in this world. I had practiced them for some time before finding success. I will include here some notes written at the time of my first encounter with my new Teacher:

From the notebook:

I wanted to know how to project my inner self to another point somewhere on the planet. Not astral projection but what was called Soul travel. I had tried the exercises given in the course and books but experienced little except a feeling of lightness.

After a session of contemplation late one evening I decided to go to bed. I asked for some proof that I had found the path my Teacher told me of. I closed my eyes and all at once I was standing at the top of a tall building that I knew was being built downtown. I could feel the wind blowing, and I looked down the side of the building to the blue neon light formed in the shape of a company logo. I could see all of downtown. Something struck me on the right arm and I opened my eyes to find I was back in the bed. I had done it! It was so real, all my senses were there on the top of the building. My wife had turned over in her sleep and brushed against my arm, bringing my attention back to my body. I did not see my Teacher, but He must have helped me to do this.

Before awakening the past within me, or I should say before I had recall of past lives, I was working with information that I knew but could not tell you how I knew it. Many passages I read in His books would take the voice of someone I knew, as if living a distant memory. It was only after months of trying to contact Him that I gave an ultimatum: if You are there, You know that I am trying to reach you. If You exist, help me now.

Nothing happened. I slumped further into the sofa that lazy afternoon and fell asleep while thinking about my failure. I looked up and remarked to myself that I needed to try a different approach, when I realized that I was sitting in a grove of trees beside a sand path. I had never seen this place, and being somewhat adventuresome, I started in the only direction that seemed to make sense.

I was totally absorbed in that moment and did not associate with my body being on the sofa. I was walking a path in a direction that seemed to call me to it.

The colors were more crisp and immediate than I had ever seen. The forest seemed endless, and I think it is, but within moments I was standing in front of a simple lean-to constructed of limbs and brush. It struck me as being quite in place there and I began making mental notes on how it was built. A voice from inside the shelter startled me.

"You are looking for something?" a man said. He half stood up around the edge of the lean-to, looked at me and grunted, then He went back inside.

"Well, no, not really," I weakly answered.

"I suppose you're searching for a Teacher who can answer all your questions," said the voice inside the hut. I then realized that I wasn't hearing the voice with my ears, but rather I could hear Him from inside of me.

I gathered my wits and replied, "Yes, I want to meet you. May I come in?"

There was no reply. I knew that I would have to pursue this conversation so I peered inside. He was a slight, simple looking man, clean shaven, wearing loose fitting pants and a pale shirt. He then looked directly at me and said, "I can't give you that, I doubt anyone can."

I wasn't sure what to do next. I wasn't sure who He was or if I should be standing there. I started to walk away when He stood up and said, "I am just another one marveling at the wonders of these worlds. You are much like me, you are living and experiencing everything right now. And I ask you, what else is there?"

I remember it seeming so simple just then, standing in the middle of an endless forest with nothing important but what was right in front of me.

He asked me to join Him, and we sat on the sandy floor

of the simple hut. I asked Him if He lived there, and laughing He told me that He was taking a walk Himself and decided to rest there for a while. There was an uncomfortable silence while He looked at me curiously. At last He invited me to speak my mind.

I searched for the words but there weren't any that expressed what I was feeling. There was so much I wanted to know, yet I shook my head.

"You know, if you spend your time wondering about what you don't know then you risk missing what is right before you now!" I just stared at the ground. As He spoke again I looked into His eyes hoping to judge if there was truth in what He was saying.

"No one can give you answers or teach you the spiritual path. You do this for yourself by living each moment. What you seek is knowledge. Knowledge cannot be taught, it must be realized. One of my Teachers told me that it must be caught! Do you know how we come to *know?*"

I shook my head again.

"Knowledge is the product of two elements, being half information and half experience. I call this knowledge, some call it wisdom. We won't argue over words. You may experience a situation in your life and not understand the meaning of it until you read a passage in a book and then—it all makes sense! You combined your personal experience with new information needed to complete the process of realization. Or you may hear a statement and not understand the meaning of it until you experience an incident that brings the point across.

"Knowledge, to *know.* Very simple, you see, information from any source plus your experience equals knowledge. Of course, it has to be the right information with the right experience!"

I wasn't sure of what he was saying.

"It's not as slipshod as it sounds. There's an exacting balance to the process really. The point is I can not answer your questions. I can only offer you information. If you apply this to your life you may realize truth that you did not know before.

"Most people think lightly on the most profound sub-jects and they base their opinions largely on what others have said. The technology of today allows for information to cross the oceans in seconds, and everyone has access to almost any subject they desire. What they do with that infor-mation is what we are discussing here.

"The data can roll around in their minds and they can formulate surface opinions on any subject, based on opi-nions of others. How often does anyone really take the time to personally explore the pros and cons of an issue, to take this information and apply it to their own moments of ex-perience? If more effort were given to the process of deciding what we personally know, then we would truly *know* more than we could believe."

It made sense to me then, overwhelming sense. I've walk-ed the sandy path many times since first meeting Him, and that road has become a symbol of His first discourse to me. The way of knowledge, if you will.

After He explained how we come to *know* I felt a need to ponder over everything He had said. I stood up and He nod-ded. As I turned to go He said to me, "One way to begin the spiritual journey is to find out where you fit in."

"You mean find out who I am?" I asked.

"You already know who you are. You are Soul. Find out where you came from, how you relate here, what your pur-pose is, and where you are going!"

I was dumbfounded and I must have looked it. He laugh-ed and said, "You wanted a challenge. It's not too much to ask, is it?"

He continued laughing quietly to Himself as I slowly started walking in the thick grove of trees. Faintly I could hear His voice inside me saying, "Step by step, moment by moment, you are unfolding with each breath you take. You have been on the path for many thousands of years. Be yourself, be all you are each moment. That is the secret you will forever hold."

As I was listening to His voice I realized that I was staring at a sliver of moonlight dancing across the edge of the sofa.

9

Past Lives

As I sat in the theatre with a box of popcorn and a cola I was not prepared for the opening scenes. I had come to see the movie *Siddartha,* based on the book by Hermann Hesse, though I had not then read the book. The opening scenes showed the landscapes of a town in India and my pulse immediately quickened. I knew that place, I had been there, but how was this possible?

The film was the story of a young man and his friend who set out to gain knowledge on the spiritual path. They both came from a good social background of respected religious families but gave that up to pursue truth in a most simple life. They searched together for some time, then they parted in the difference of understanding. Siddartha decided that he had reached a plateau of knowledge and saw no reason not to experience the life of material gains. Many years later they meet again as Siddartha returns to his spiritual quest.

The movie was filmed in India and produced in a careful and sensitive manner, unusual in the vast libraries of commercial movies.

As I sat watching the film I not only recognized the landscapes, I saw so much of my own search in the story. There were scenes that I remember being in the film that I could not find when I saw it again a few years later. In reading the book those scenes were not there. They were my scenes, out of my past, and I confused them with those in the film when seeing it for the first time.

As the movie ended I sat still in my seat until everyone else had left. Tears were running down my cheeks. I had revisited a part of me that I didn't mentally know was there. Over the next few days many memories surfaced, but I could not be sure of their place in my life. I had crossed a bridge inside of me, one that spanned this life with my past. In the next several years, with much effort, I was able to knowingly tap into the past at will.

I still think back to times in the East with great affection, as I have lived many lifetimes in that region. I did meet several of my Masters there for the first time and studied some of the basic teachings. At one time the East was the center of spiritual awareness on this planet, and it was only natural that Soul would be born into that area if It needed the experience of those situations. While there are still Masters working and living in the East, the Western world is now the spiritual center with the United States being the greatest current-day influence in spiritual teaching.

There was also sadness of growing pains in the past, and I had to learn to balance what I was uncovering. It is possible to trace every life we have lived, though there is little to gain in that exhaustive effort. It is more important to realize the essence of where we have been.

Reincarnation is widely misunderstood, and this stems from altered and errored accounts of Eastern thought. You will not be born again as an animal, no matter how many people tell you that at cocktail parties and New Age seminars. So great is the misconception that I choose to not use the word reincarnation any more than necessary.

Soul gains experience by using outer coverings, or bodies, to live in each environment. Much of the learning process for Soul takes place on this plane of awareness and others in the Lower Worlds. Life after life, from one body to another, Soul lives the experiences of the time in order to gain spiritual experience. Spiritual experience can be thought of as being the essence and ultimate truth behind the moment to moment life experiences which provide conditions for spiritual truth to be realized.

Soul retains all Its experiences but does not carry them as a mental memory. Soul does not live in any moment but the present, and it does not relate directly to past or future. It accepts that cultures have conditioned thinking to provide for things that have happened and those that may happen, but it does not usually concern itself with these concepts. Why should It? All It knows is what is *now,* because *now* is all that Soul ever has control over. What we call past is known to be a present factor of experience for Soul; neither good, bad, long ago or recent. It is all part of the ongoing experience. Soul does not die when the body does; It does not lose awareness for a second. It accepts the conditions of the lives and experiences, but It knows that only one factor matters . . . what is at hand *now.*

By developing awareness of our own past lives, which involves tapping into Soul awareness, we can find clues that will explain conditions that exist for us today. We may see how decisions made three hundred years ago effect us now, which is the action/reaction of karma. We can carry a fear or attachment today that practically rules our lives and find the source in an event long ago in the past, and, therefore, the potential for its correction. This is a useful purpose for examining past lives.

Problems may arise when we have the awareness to see our past but do not yet have the understanding to see how the events relate to what is ultimately important. We have all been through the most foolish and humiliating of times; just as we have been bold, we have also allowed ourselves to have been victimized. It is a normal part of the life experience, and the lessons often are repeated many times before we choose not to go through them again. When we examine a life we may be shocked to see the conditions we endured, and we can easily become depressed. There is a thought that is worth considering, and that is that whatever you went through to get here, you are *here!* And this isn't a bad place to be! What we have experienced has made us who we are now, and that is a reality everyone must face personally.

I have had people tell me that they create problems for themselves by getting involved with people that they feel they have known in the past. When asked why they were drawn into the relationship, they conclude that it was to reconnect a missing part of their lives or to finish unsettled business. It was a problem because they had really wanted to take another course, but felt compelled to explore the past.

It is not unusual for us to be sharing this life with Souls we have dealt with in the past. We may find them in family relationships more than anywhere else, and this is to provide us with the opportunity to balance the karmic conditions between us. We may meet a complete stranger and feel like we know that person. Perhaps we do, perhaps we don't. Often your vibratory rate harmonizes with another's rate and you can mistake this for a past relationship. Be discriminating and base your relationships on sound judgments, making a knowing decision.

Past lives represent a mystery to almost everyone who accepts the possibility of it being true. We love a mystery, and we feel compelled to dive into the adventure and romance of our own past. Upon examination we can find it to be much more mundane than we anticipated. What we call the past is just a record of where we have been. Nothing more and nothing less. It has a purpose, and looking into and understanding our past is part of the development of Soul. We should explore past lives with an openness, and yet with a balance in relating it to our life today.

I would advise you to not depend on others to tell you about your past. Those that know how to read the past and understand the spiritual implications are few and far between. There are people who deceive you outright, but most readers believe they can help you. Usually they are tapping into their own past, not yours, and they don't realize the difference. There are those who can read the past of others, but they are picking up images from the causal body, or awareness. The causal, or seed body, contains parts of the past but is largely incomplete. A Master is capable of knowing your past if you request that He become involved, but more often He will help you to discover it for yourself. More important than just knowing the events of the past He can guide you into realizing the causes and effects as they relate to your awareness now.

Hypnosis is used to provide past life regression, and it does work for many people. They see their past, or I should say that they often relive their past. There is a major difference in being an observer and being a participant. Because those people working with hypnosis do not generally understand all the implications involved, they suggest that you regress into the life experience. This may put you into the first person experience again, complete with the information and emotions felt at that time. If you were regressing to find you were a Christian being thrown to the lions, you would re-experience the terror and pain of those moments. This can lead to severe problems in the here and now.

If a Master were to get involved He may likely write down or tell you about your past. If He helped you to witness the past you would be an observer, much like seeing a movie. Seeing these images may provoke great senses of memory or knowing and may stir emotions in you, but they are the emotions of *now* balanced with stability of your total awareness. If you search out your past be an observer, not a participant.

An excellent way to explore past lives is through the dream state. As you are going to sleep give yourself the suggestion that you will be able to observe a select part of your past. If you sense certain places or events try to find out more about them. If you are beginning your search and don't know what to explore, suggest to yourself that you explore the area that has greatest significance to you now.

The dream process may take time. You have to condition yourself to follow the suggestions and to retain the information in your conscious mind. Keep a notebook beside the bed, and when you awake after a dream write the experience down right then. Over time you will begin to see patterns in your dreams. When you read them in the notebook you will draw into your memory details you may have forgotten, and by this you are training the outer consciousness to remain open to your inner experiences. Whether you're searching for answers in the past or wanting to better understand your dreams, keeping a bedside diary will help.

If you are working with a Master, ask for assistance. You will be shown what you need as you are able to handle the information. This is usually a slower pace than we would take if we had our way, but this is to protect us from taking in experience at a faster rate than we are able to digest. If we cannot learn from the experience, then why go through it? A Master will pace you so as to get maximum benefit from minimum effort. That's the way of the spiritual worlds.

10

Out
of the Body

I was reading books and discourses on all the secrets that I had wondered about being true. Did I first hear them in my dreams or did my Teacher tell me about them? I could not remember. But written on those pages were passages I had heard before; concepts never expressed to me except somewhere deep within.

I was consumed by the flow of Spirit working through me, and in truth it was all I could do to work my job. I would use the day to best earn the living, but I really lived for the evenings of quiet contemplation.

This involved sitting in a still room, the lights dim or out, and breathing deeply to relax. Then I would slowly begin to chant a spiritual word, gradually breathing the word out louder and then bringing the sound back in to myself. Many spiritually charged words have two syllables, the first one chanted with the breath out, the second one chanted with the breath in. There are many words that can be used, most common are the names of GOD, or it could be the name of your Teacher, though mine frowned on that. If you work with a Master ask for a spiritual word to use. If you are not aware of a Teacher in your life then ask Spirit to provide one. If you are at a point where this would serve you then you will receive it.

After ten to twenty rounds of chanting the word I would

sit in silence and most often my body would be vibrating with the sound still inside me. This actually raises your vibratory rate, with certain words carrying a higher catalytic effect than others. Often I could still hear the sound moving within me though my voice was silent.

Taught in a number of studies is to learn to see with your inner sight. I would focus my attention on a spot several inches above my nose, a spot often called the "Third Eye." Soul is said to rest near that spot, and there is a basis of fact in that, but concentrating attention there did little more than give me a headache. I found that relaxing my attention and allowing it to flow worked wonders. Often I would shift my awareness to a completely different location and suddenly realize what I had done, quickly jolting back to the body sitting in the dark.

These exercises were designed to help regain contact with the inner self, to put aside the outside worries and distractions and meditate on more spiritual thoughts. Many groups use a technique similar to this. A better concept is one of contemplation, which suggests a more detached attitude than meditation. When we meditate we easily can concentrate on an image or idea, and will usually build a wall around that image, not allowing Soul to connect with the mind. By contemplating a thought we view it from a detached viewpoint and examine it, but we do not focus all our attention on it. We are fluid and drift into other areas. If we find a spot we like, we pause to examine it; then we move on again. The inner worlds are more easily realized when we relax our attention from the mind and body and flow in the natural rhythm inside of us. In doing this we are leaving the body awareness and exploring the inner realities.

Remember the first few days of spring when you were in high school? You used to sit and stare out the window and you were a million miles away, completely unaware of the teacher repeatedly calling your name. This is daydreaming, and really no different than night dreaming except that we put our physical world consciousness on pause with our eyes open instead of shut. Where do you go when you daydream, do you remember a time from the past, do you imagine a new place you've never been before? How do we do this?

"It's just your imagination," the adults would say, and you've probably said it to kids, too. But what is imagination? Everything, all matter, all being is a part of GOD, there can be no exceptions to this. Everything you hold inside is your reality, your truth, and no one knows this better than you do. How can one part of us be less real than another part? Isn't all of our awareness important? The truth is that daydreaming is simply shifting awareness from the physical outer surrounding to another awareness within us. Both realms are viewed; both are seen, heard, felt, smelled, and real in the moment we are aware of them. The reason daydreaming is discounted is because you can't put your physical sense on it. What an old world attitude, "I won't believe it until I see it." We start out as children being taught what is real and what is not, and most of us have been told that our imaginations aren't reality. As explorers on the spiritual path we must learn to recognize the concepts that others have implanted in us and replace them with conclusions based on our own experiences. If you want to shift your awareness "out of your body" and into another realm you simply let go of where you are and come into agreement with where you want to be.

The more you think about leaving this awareness the harder it is, so relax your attitude when you contemplate. Drift in the moment, forget the details of the day and go with the current that always flows inside you. I used to sit in contemplation for a half hour or so and usually fall asleep somewhere in the process.

One night, after studying the written discourses for just over a year, I fell asleep while wondering about my place in all of this. I became aware of standing up in front of the couch I was leaning on while contemplating. The room was still dark. My Master was to my left, pointing to dozens of multicolored lines that ran from one piece of furniture to another, and He told me that everything was connected to everything else. As He was saying this I felt an understanding take place, and I carried the thought further and realized that all the planes of action were interconnected. My actions in the physical could impact on my astral, causal and mental bodies. He then told me that there was a vibratory awareness that was coarser than the physical realm Soul actively dealt with, and yet many of our actions here utilized this field. A sudden impulse told me that He was referring to some of the metaphysical techniques.

At that point I lost my head completely and openly doubted my Master. I said, "Oh, I don't know if that's true!" There was silence. I froze when I turned to face Him. I looked at the web of colored threads connecting everything before me, and the lines were running from my hands to where I pointed. I said, "If everything is connected then I want to draw from this energy to heal my knees, they've given me much pain." I had injured them in an accident.

The Master said nothing in response and I suddenly awoke leaning against the couch, the room very dark. I replayed my experience a dozen times in my mind, and I knew I had stepped over the line this time. I went to bed still thinking about my blunder, but when I got up the next morning my knees didn't hurt.

We needed more money with a new baby in the house, so I took on a morning paper route. I worked my regular job from eight in the morning until six in the evening, ate dinner and saw the family, went to bed at nine at night to get up at one-thirty in the morning for the route. It was an interesting time of learning to get by on just a few hours sleep. The city was dead that time of the morning, and the solitude was refreshing. I'd finish about six in the morning, go home and shower, and head for the donut shop for one and coffee. Then I drove to my regular job and the day began again. There really was no time for contemplation, but with less sleep I found myself a little out of the normal mind set I was used to. I could project myself to another awareness and back without effort, and this amused me.

Hutch and I would meet once a week when I called on him, allowing fifteen minutes for business and the hour lunch break for the most interesting conversations in the city. We were both wanting to tap into the Soul awareness, where it was said that everything could be known because Soul would then be in complete awareness of Itself. This is, in fact, a flawed conclusion because Soul will only know what It knows, not necessarily everything there is to know, but we were working on that angle at the time. We did a lot of probing aloud and challenged each other to take many steps that might not have been taken if studying alone. Hutch had a lot of experiences that I marveled at, and in many ways I credit him with helping me to see a new reality. He, too, had spent a time having to work several jobs and not getting much sleep.

I had ordered a glazed donut and black coffee to go and was sitting in my car early one winter morning. I took a sip and as I set the cup down on the dash I felt dizzy and I lost consciousness. I then became aware of complete lightness, as if I had no form or being, and I was thinking without thought process; I was just *knowing*. I then realized that I was in Soul awareness and I could learn whatever I wanted to know. I was on the Soul plane! So what questions did I have? Surprise, I had none. No questions. Then I drifted.

A moment later I opened my eyes and in the next second tried desperately to hold on to what I had found, to bring that information back with me into my mind. Most of it slipped through my grasp; there were no mental images of where I had been, and yet I *knew* where I had been. I sensed the knowledge, but I could not remember it. I reached for the coffee, still dazed at the experience, and found it cold. I was just gone a minute, but the clock said it was eight-thirty. I had been sitting there for forty-five minutes and it seemed to be just one. Needless to say I couldn't tell my boss why I was late to work, and for some unknown reason he didn't ask. As I was sneaking in the back of the building it occurred to me why I didn't have any questions when I was on the Soul plane. I remembered what my Teacher had told me about the answers to my questions, "When you see enough in life to look for the next step you are walking on familiar ground." When I was there I *knew* the answers instantly upon being part of that awareness, so I had no questions. The answer to every Lower World question does lie in Soul awareness, but one must first be aware of the question. If you are aware of the question then you have probably realized the answer in

Soul awareness but have not yet realized it mentally. If you are not aware of the question to ask then you will not search for an answer. Soul is aware of much more than the mind can or will accept, and many questions we pose mentally are the promptings of Soul to uncover a new understanding in our minds.

It then occurred to me that the trick was to bring some of the information back, to break the barrier between Soul and the mind, and that was a challenge I worked on for many months.

But why did it seem that I was gone a minute when forty-five minutes passed? Because there is no time on the Soul plane, only in the Lower Worlds. I could have been there for centuries and had no awareness of time because it does not exist there, and yet the clock ticks on in the physical!

A few weeks later we had our first snow of the season. I was rounding the corner of an apartment building with a bundle of papers in my arms when a very sharp pain in my right knee sent me sprawling. When I tried to get up my other knee went out, and there I was, four in the morning and in worse pain than before. And lying in the snow with two hours worth of deliveries to make. I got the point real quick. Everything was connected and I had used the lower vibratory power to temporarily mend my knees. My Master allowed me to do this on my own. I was in a state of awareness to accomplish many things that evening and I wasted it on something selfish. At that moment I felt a billion miles from the Soul plane, and yet I knew I had probably taken another step forward in my new realization in the snow. Now if I could just get up and get on with my work! Eventually I did manage to hobble around to complete the route. My knees bothered me for years, and they were made even worse by rock climbing periodically. It was a burden I carried for a long time, and I remember when I finished with it. The score was eventually settled, and today I rarely feel any pain there.

11

Do You Remember?

The grey mist was held to the ground by the cool air that swept through the peaks of the snowcapped mountains. I was watching the rising sun splinter its brilliant rays behind a rock formation and fill the green valley with yellow and orange light. The boulder I sat upon was cupped from the force of thousands of years of ice and heat, but that morning it humbly served as a spot for reflection.

"It hasn't changed in appearance," He said. "Do you remember when we last were here?"

My mind was heavy with the thoughts that would not clear, and my heart felt again the confusion of once having to leave this place. I looked directly into His eyes and I *knew* our past together, but I could not recall the details.

"I always called you Master and I know our purpose together, but I cannot recall your name."

"Names are used only in these worlds. While sometimes they seem important in the images of our lives, names hold no place of value in the Higher Worlds. We simply *know* each other.

"We have the name given at birth, and sometimes this name comes close to reflecting our awareness. I'm speaking of the vibratory rate of the words themselves. If you have to live in the world with a name that sounds coarse and heavy to you then you might be happier to find one that better harmonizes with you.

"Sometimes a Master will give you a spiritual name which will be highly charged and help to accelerate your growth. At times your spiritual name will be the name you carried in a past incarnation, perhaps a life that held great realization for you.

"A Master can use any name that suits Him, but often it is the last Lower World name he held, if He likes it. Many years ago I had the name Azjur Ramini and it is a name I often use now."

Suddenly I remembered, though the thought was still far away. I recognized the sound of His name and the image of Him standing in my living room eight years earlier, overlayed with the sound of His name being repeated in my mind.

I suddenly realized that I was staring directly at Him, where in other experiences I was only aware of His presence. I was not surprised at His appearance but I wondered why I had not looked at Him before. He was tall, about six feet, clean shaven and trim, though He appeared strong. His skin was dark, as was His hair, and He wore a simple brown robe that fell to His knees, with a knotted belt made of twine, or cloth.

He knew my thoughts.

"I see that you remember. Little has changed in appearances with this valley or with me.

"We know each other well, I can tell you that, but you already know it. You were observing in most of the travels we have been on, and now you are participating. You are using your energy to move and see what is around you."

I looked at myself and I was astonished. I was wearing a dark brown robe, much like His.

"We can take the appearance of the attitude we carry, the feelings we choose to express. With practice you can appear as you please in the Lower Worlds. You are now touching that area of awareness we can call the past, and you appeared then much like you appear now. Do you feel any different?"

My thoughts seemed like a stone skipping across a still pond. I would catch glimpses of the two of us together and then the image changed, each time taking me further into the distant memory.

"Do you appear like this now, or is this how you appeared then?" I asked.

"I've chosen to appear this way, even now. The choice is mine. I can change to suit the need of the situation. While here working in the Lower World I need to use a body, and this is the one I've had for some time. I'd probably look silly in a suit, wouldn't I?"

I listened to what He was saying, but my memory was still racing on the edge of a discovery. Then I *knew*.

"Yes, I first met you on the road. You knew me but I had not seen you before. I was walking toward a village to find information on a Master; some said He lived here." I looked around me and recognized the landscape.

He smiled and then said, "You and I spent a great deal of time together here. I first told you of how your true Self *knows* and your mind thinks, while your emotions feel no different than everyone else. You had a great opinion of yourself at times. You believed you had the key to heaven, but you dared not to use it."

I did recall those fears, they had been with me for what seemed like forever. I looked at Him again and I wondered why we were discussing me.

"You chose to leave here and return to your learning. You had traveled with me to some of the hidden worlds, and you wanted to know more. Why did you leave?"

He was challenging me to acknowledge the decisions I had made. I had asked Him a year earlier for help in remembering my last life. He had taken me further back in time to the previous life to that one, and I never dreamed it could be such a challenge. I did remember the feelings and they were at first painful, and then they seemed as if they were someone else's feelings. I felt an odd detachment, even though I was thinking of myself.

I slowly began to speak. "I wanted to be like you and I couldn't. I tried and I wanted the experience but it would not come. I was empty and it seemed that I had found all the conclusions of my existence. I don't think I had a choice. I was not ready."

"Rasheen, you were the most eager of my chelas. You had great promise, and yet you decided you were not ready. In your mind you had reasoned GOD, and in your emotions you wanted IT more than anything else. You wanted IT too much; you had a desire that could not be satisfied then. You could no longer hold that frustration inside so you returned to the world of men. Did you find your release?"

I knew that I had not, but I could not answer.

"Look inside to where you were."

I closed my eyes and saw my death coming a few years after leaving Him. I felt nothing as I watched the scenes change.

There was a pause and then I saw the man I was in the next life, recognizing him immediately. I had suspected this, but now the life was proven before me. It was sad. I wanted GOD and as a poet I wrote of that desire and the struggle of man to balance the forces of nature and spirit and the purpose of the struggle. Yet, I could not balance my own life, and I hid behind the image of the poet and his madness. I died not speaking with my Master in that life; I had not made contact with Him. I had chosen to find the answers for myself in the outside world only to suffer in the questions.

When I opened my eyes, He was standing directly in front of me staring into my eyes. He looked through me with His timeless expression. I didn't feel the sadness and I didn't have any more questions about my past. I was only aware of Him watching me and then of the cold breeze on my face.

"You knew the information you sought when you and I were on this spot last, but you did not have the experience to balance your life. Your desire was your attachment, and you have seen the way of the weighted path. When we want something too much we push it away; when we do not pursue it at all it will not come to us either. If we fear it, we bring it to us without fail; but in the fear we will never realize the positive aspect. The answer is not to fear it, not to want it to an extreme, but to pursue it with a casual but consistant interest. This is the middle path. This is the way to GOD and all things in the spiritual worlds.

"You are Soul and throughout this life you have been working on the balance. You began this life knowing the goal and the challenge, and you wanted to find out about everything spiritual from the start. Nothing has held your interest for long because you knew deep within you the truth of what we discussed so long ago."

"You are right, of course. Much of this is overwhelming. I've wanted to understand this for so long. Will I be able to remember what we are discussing?" I asked.

"You will know what you have seen, and the memory images will slowly come into your conscious mind awareness. You will keep with you always the experience. You have only to fully realize who you are."

"I am nothing compared to who I will be one day," I said quietly.

"You are whole now in that you have all the abilities needed to be the Master. You have only to realize your awareness and your place, balance your powers, and *be* in the worlds of GOD."

"I know that I create my own world, and I'm not satisfied with what I use in my life."

"Creation is finished for all material and Lower World planes of awareness. You do not create your world; you become aware of another part of you. There is nothing new; there is only what you are not yet aware of. If you insist on holding on to structures of past and future, structures of what is good and bad and images of what is or is not, then you will not see who you are now. The secret is letting go of all these illusions and seeing yourself as Soul, *now.* The spiritual experience is known in *being, now,* in complete awareness of the moment. Come with me."

The mountains faded in the wisps of thin clouds, and then the vision was a starry sky, a universe of life with no one world within reach.

The mist enveloped us once more and when it cleared I could sense the presence of the Master, but He appeared as a globe of energy, a brilliant sphere of yellow light. The landscape was vast and flooded with a soft, pale light that did not come from any one direction and did not allow shadows. When I looked down at myself I appeared much like Him, though not as brilliant.

I sensed His voice; actually I knew His words within me.

"This is who you are, Soul. This is where you know your Self, the knowledge of yourself and *being here, now.*"

We seemed to move, but we were not walking, nor were we really moving. It was my viewpoint that changed. I was aware of a tremendous building and of being inside of it.

"I wanted you to know your place in this world, not just where you have been, but where you can always be. Do you see the wall before you?"

I was aware of a wall that appeared to be marble, but it glistened with a golden light. There were no symbols or images on the wall and yet as I fixed my attention on it I seemed to become aware of a history, but it was told from a present point of view. I moved closer to the wall and I understood.

I awoke that morning with a great sense of knowing, but I could not remember any details. I sat on the edge of the bed and stared at the pattern of the Persian rug on the floor.

Looking about the room I saw several volumes of books on the desk and one under the stack seemed to stand out. Reaching for it my palms burned as I picked it up. It was a book of poems I read often, and in seeing this I uttered, "Oh, God," realizing then what I had endured in the past life. When I was a young man, in the first year of high school, the English teacher introduced me to that volume of poetry, and to that poet. In reading the lines then I recognized the thoughts and images that created the work, though I did not understand that at the time. After reading just the first line of a poem I could quote most of the other lines. Now I understood why.

Throughout the following week I felt a lightness from time to time, and an inner sense of awareness, but nothing specific.

Life went on; the job and the family filled my time and I tried to take each day as it came.

I arrived home from work one day and had a few hours

of silence before the family would return from a trip to the country. Staring out to the field behind the house, I watched the birds settle in the trees as the sun fell behind the low clouds. My mind turned over the thoughts I was struggling with. I thirsted for more information, but books would not satisfy my need to know. I reflected on the questions I had, the answers I thought might be true, and the inner sense of some purpose to this period in my life. I stretched out on the couch and slowly drifted to sleep.

I became aware of standing beside Ramini, but someone else was explaining a new concept to me and several others, though I did not see their faces. He was dark skinned, dressed in a short red and black robe, tied in the middle with a rope. He was of medium build and height, and wore a closely trimmed beard. I later learned that His name is Rebazar.

Sweeping His arm over an imaginary image of a man, He explained, "There are fourteen bands of Self to be realized. Some call these band initiations, but this is only partially correct. The bands are areas of awareness, and each one of you will spend a period of experience in each one. As the experience builds on itself your vibratory action will be higher, and you will carry your life into the next band of awareness. Is this clear?

"You are beginning the path in the first band, and you are making your emotional choices in the second. The third will expose you to your past action, and the fourth will challenge your mind to balance. The fifth is the awareness of the true Self, Soul, and you are among the few to have walked this far. The sixth is the balancing of the Self in these worlds, the seventh is the study of the powers behind the power. The eighth is the dark night of Soul in these worlds, and all the worlds, as you will now be alone in your journey to GOD. The ninth is the journey into the heavens to prove IT ALL, the tenth is having first found an aspect of IT. The eleventh is probing deeper into the heart of IT, and the twelfth is becoming one with IT, ITSELF. You are now the Master. The thirteenth is a broader realization of IT and the work in all the worlds of GOD, and the fourteenth is the unspeakable realization within GOD.

"In this, I have said nothing that can be held as absolute, yet I have spoken the truth that applies to your consciousness. How does one sum up the path to GOD in a few words? Go about your life and find these levels in your experience."

I awoke with a heavy fog over my thoughts. After a few minutes I could recall vividly the image of the Teacher, and then slowly His words came to me. I scribbled notes on the essence of what He said, and then I remembered having read about the levels of awareness in a book. Finding the section I found reference to only seven levels, yet the Teacher referred to fourteen. Why?

This kept me busy thinking for months, but the answer to the mystery came many years later.

12

The
True Self

There is one center in each of us, and surrounding that
center are the common and most used facets of our daily
lives. All of us have minds, emotions, and bodies in various
conditions and areas of development. Science commonly
credits our mind with being the outstanding feature that
separates us but it is not.

Religions have referred to it for thousands of years, but
today there is not one in twenty million who could tell you
that they know intimately about it. What is that center?

Soul. Mystery has surrounded It; yet It is the spark of life
in every one of us. We would not be who we are without It.

The tale of Adam and Eve symbolizes in some ways the
creation of Soul and the worlds of GOD, primarily the
material plane. We also have the records in the Great Halls of
Knowledge found on the Soul plane itself, and these tell of
the reasons and methods used to form the worlds we know.
There are only a few beings who experienced the transition
period itself, and they support the records in every detail.

GOD ITSELF exists as an energy; at least this is the
closest thought representation we can have of IT. There have
been personifications of IT over the ages, and there are
limited manifestations or representatives of IT on the various
planes. Beyond the highest worlds that can be discussed and
written of IT exists as a formless, unlimited, all inclusive

energy. The records indicate that IT has always been and will be, for time too was a creation of IT.

Soul was brought forth from GOD ITSELF, and is a part of that SUPREME BEING. Everything that exists is part of IT, but a special spark was given to the form of Soul. The term "Son of God" referred to in the Bible as being the Christ is in fact a reference to Soul being a part of GOD, each of us as Soul being the offspring of GOD. Jesus was shown this reality before He made public His ministry and viewed Himself as a humble being, a Soul as having recognized His position in the worlds of GOD. Many of the concepts Jesus is reported to have expressed have been viewed as Christ referring to Himself in a singular, personal manner. Jesus most often used Himself as an example of one Soul who was like each Soul in the worlds of GOD and did not see Himself as being greater in any way than another Soul. Most of the world saviours have expressed their teachings by personal example but realized the actual relationship of Soul to GOD.

The purpose for Soul is to experience the worlds and discover for Itself Its true home, to learn the spiritual wisdom of GOD, and return to *know* IT. Soul begins aware of very little and enters the first series of bodies It will inhabit. Over thousands of years Soul learns from the lessons of the lives It endures and one day becomes aware of a greater power than Itself. Many, many lives later It becomes aware of Itself outside of the body form, as Soul, and then begins the final steps of the journey to realize GOD ITSELF.

All of this sounds simplistic written here, but there are no words that can relate this truth. We are also challenged by the logical nature of our minds which insist on trying to second guess the reasoning of GOD. Every religious study must contend with the unanswerable questions of why GOD would create us just to go through what IT already knew existed. And why would IT make us suffer to know IT? There are many who feel that we are little more than puppets on strings, dancing to the cosmic tunes of an unknown fiddler. I can relate well to these thoughts; they are the questions of us all at one time or another.

All I can offer you is the most basic information. I am not

avoiding the issue by saying that everyone must prove this reality for themselves and come into an understanding of it. It is not possible to know the truth behind the creation while dealing in the confines of the Lower Worlds. Yet each Soul can *know* the truth by working into that position of actively working in the Higher Worlds. I will not insult you by offering complicated explanations and theories. It is my experience that the most profound truths of all existence can be the simplest in realization. I guess that's part of the test too. We look for the logical or complicated reasons when usually the most basic and simple reason lies before us. One basic premise of the Higher Worlds is the reality that All simply IS, no more and no less. The Higher Worlds or GOD Worlds reality just IS; there is no logic or mental gymnastics to master. There are many worlds of GOD, and they are divided basically into two areas, the Higher Worlds and the Lower Worlds. An area commonly called the Soul Plane is the center line, though it lies just within the Higher Worlds. Soul experiences the needed realizations by inhabiting bodies in all of these worlds. Every world has a different vibratory rate and therefore a different body form for Soul to use. The vibratory rate of Soul can be thought of as being very high, and when in a world beneath the Soul plane It must be protected by an outer covering or body. Soul will continue from world to world, life to life, until It realizes Itself and knowingly chooses to return to Its true home. The mental body is the first covering of Soul, then the causal, the astral, and the material body.

Soul is the innermost part of each of us. It is who we really are. When the rigid patterns of the mind don't block It out, It speaks and directs our actions. But for thousands of lives, Soul is virtually imprisoned within the other bodies. It is not strong or experienced enough to affect the actions that would lead it closer to GOD. It is not even aware of Itself until nearing the end of Its journey. Once we know who we are and recognize the potential we truly have, then we can change everything before us.

Soul can be thought of as a child, learning through the experiences It goes through in all the lifetimes. As It grows in awareness, It grows stronger and more knowledgeable. Some have said that Soul is all-knowing, but It must grow into that position. It can reach a point of being able to tap into the resources of the Soul plane, where all can be known that concerns the worlds below it.

Soul is by nature a happy being; It is not subject to the emotions and mental stresses except when trapped in the bodies It must carry in these worlds. Thankfully we can learn to temporarily drop these other bodies and spend time on the plane of our choosing.

Every Soul is made up of a part of GOD, yet It is different from any other Soul. It has been offered a path of Its own, a will that can be expressed at the pace and manner that suits It.

There are two main divisions of the creation, the Higher Worlds and the Lower Worlds or planes. We think of the planes as being stacked, but in truth they are not. Just as light, temperature, and sound may simultaneously exist at the same time in a room, the planes co-exist within the other. Each plane has a band of vibratory action that differs from the others, and one seldom interferes with the next.

There are two main facets of the Lower Worlds. Each world has areas that Soul experiences or lives a period of time in a so-called body in order to learn the lessons needed for the individual. Each plane is also made up of a primary essence, and it is this that we also carry with us minute to minute in our awareness.

The material world is made up of the universes of matter and contains worlds of beings, the Earth and its people are part of this. There are laws that concern only the material world, and our bodies and forms are subject to them.

The astral, or emotional plane is comprised of thousands of varying sub-planes as are all of the worlds. There are life forms there, usually unaware of any world but their own. There are some astral beings who can affect the physical worlds if aided by sympathetic Souls who draw their presence. Our emotions are based on the essence of the astral world, and we carry this essence with us here and now.

The material world is a dim reflection of the astral, but is a reflection all the same. Many of our dreams take place in the astral awareness or you can say the astral world; and the landscapes and images we see, feel, hear and sense are similar to those on this planet. The most apparent evidence of being in the astral awareness is the vividness of color and sensation. Often we are experiencing life in the astral awareness and do not realize it because the scenery and conditions are so similar. Sometimes the images are reversed in the astral world. Once in the dream state I was driving a small car very fast through familiar countryside when I saw that the speed limit sign was printed backward, the numbers and letters were reversed. I excitedly realized where I was and stopped the car to walk around. I approached the sign and when I touched it I awoke in my bed with my hand against the headboard. A strong shift in emotion can change your experience rapidly in astral awareness because that is part of the essence of the plane.

The causal, or seed body plane acts as a record of most of our lives of the past. This essence holds the memory and causes of actions and reactions of our lives while in the Lower Worlds. Soul also carries with it the memory of Its experiences, and when experiencing the causal world these memories can be refocused into meaningful information for the present. Soul lives within this awareness, though for less periods of time. The astral plane is a reflection of the causal awareness, except that the colors and sensations are more vivid here than on the astral.

The sub-mental, or sub-conscious plane is mentioned because we place so much importance on it in psychology. It lies very close indeed to the mental plane, and usually one is mistaken for the other. Some studies call this the etheric plane and give a separate place of being for the mental awareness. Soul experiences life in these worlds as well. The essence of these worlds is held in our own mind, and while an incredibly powerful tool; the mind is but an instrument used to help us along the way. By no means is the mind our source of knowledge or being; it is a processor and but a tool for us to use.

The subconscious mind works with images and all of our

impressions are stored in this form. If we have a good memory of a time and place, it is stored in the etheric awareness as an image, complete with all sensations involved. At some point in the future we may smell a certain perfume, or hear a song from the past, or see a forgotten place and have the memory of that special event brought back to the conscious awareness. The subconscious mind finds the similar image and replays the experience as memory by interrelating with the causal awareness. This same mechanism works on an unpleasant event too, and when we learn to fine tune our abilities we can go through experiences without being overcome by images of past similar experiences. Most fears are based on negative images, reactivated by present events that are similar to a past experience that was painful.

The mental awareness itself is based on images too, but primarily on symbols. Concepts are known by the value of the symbol represented, and often in dreams we find these symbols and do not understand their meaning. There really is no mystery; it is but the higher mental awareness expressed in the form of its origin. To understand the meaning the symbol can be impressed upon the vision of the mind's eye in contemplation and the lower mental awareness will begin to decipher the symbol into concepts (images), then thought, and into letters and words that we hear within ourselves. Some people call this inner monologue, which seems like a dialogue, the internal conversation; the mind processing and rationalizing symbols into thoughts.

Once I found myself watching an older gentleman dressed in work coveralls and a rumpled felt hat adjusting a fitting on a long pipe. When I stepped back to expand my view, I was aware of a huge geometric shape suspended in a star-filled space with the man and myself on one small part of it. I asked him what he was doing and he answered that he was doing his job! Upon further questioning he explained that he maintained an area of concepts to the specifications held by those who accepted them. When the concepts changed, he changed the image of the concept. This experience was a mock-up for me, an image of a truth held in the mental plane arranged by my Teacher.

This mental awareness has the potential for a great deal of power in the Lower Worlds. Miracles are performed by using the abilities found here and expressed in the material world.

There are Souls living in the mental realm and they are generally advanced spiritually. All the worlds below the mental plane are based on the images found in this area. The sun, the scenery, the body form, all images are dim reflections of what is found in the mental awareness.

Many world religions base their concepts of heaven on the stories of select experiences of their founders while they were visiting the mental plane. If I did not know there was more to the worlds of GOD I would assume that it was heaven, too.

Each Lower World plane has a ruler who is easily mistaken for GOD by those who do not know. They have immense power within their region and are charged with maintaining the order of the plane they oversee. Each ruler is but Soul, and the experience is another learning tool for not only the Souls who come before them, but for the rulers themselves.

The Soul plane is the first area of awareness in the Higher Worlds, and is the true home of Soul. Here Soul does not need the protective coverings of the other bodies, It can simply be in the environment of Its natural Self. This world is vast, though space is not part of the fabric of Soul awareness. Countless Souls reside here, many basking in the radiance of a true GOD world. Time does not exist here and movement is not known. There is action through *being* and awareness, and Soul continues to grow and experience on the Soul plane.

There are countless other planes above the Soul plane, and they are known by various names. I will not dwell on them here because they are to be experienced and near impossible to describe. The fifth major plane above the Soul plane is where the first true encounter with GOD ITSELF will likely take place. Yet there is no end to the worlds of GOD.

The Lower Worlds are commonly called MEST Worlds,

for matter, energy, space and time. These forms exist only in the Lower Worlds. The Higher Planes do not deal with time, space, form or matter of any type. All the images we hold of structure do not exist in the Higher Worlds because there is no need of them. In the Lower Worlds we think of movement, but in the Higher Planes there is no movement, there is no place to go. Soul simply *is,* and It has only to *be* Itself. The worlds beyond the Soul plane are explored by changing awareness into them, much like can be done in the Lower Worlds but without effort.

Think of it, no time or space, no matter or movement. This is difficult to conceive of because the mind can form an image of anything it knows, but the Higher Planes are beyond the mind and therefore unknown to it. Any image we may visualize is imperfect and based on material concepts. When Soul is in the Higher Worlds It does not need the mind, emotions or the body to use or protect It.

I have found it interesting that the Lower Worlds were formed as reflective images of each other, going down from the mental plane. Envision this Earth, the colors, the life forms. Similar images exist on the astral plane, except the colors are brighter and everything is in sharper focus. This is also true of the causal plane, and of the mental plane. Every world is but a very dim reflection of each plane above it, or lower in vibratory action. The sun that shines in the astral world is blinding to our sight here, and yet it is dim to the light source found on the mental plane.

Once we realize who we are, we begin to explore in greater depth the mysteries around us. One of the biggest fears we face in every life is death. We are born not usually aware of where we have been. It is a merciful safeguard that keeps us from being overwhelmed by our past. We have a chance to begin anew, and a chance for new experiences that may lead us to Self realization. Self realization is mistaken for an experience most often in the astral world, but true understanding of ourselves comes from *being* in the awareness of the Soul plane.

In this process we may have some memories of past lives,

and this is a natural stimulus for us to look harder for the truth of our real place in the creation.

Until we are able to act responsibly and make decisions with full awareness of the effects, we have those who assist us in choosing the next life experience. Every effort is made to match Soul with the life that will probably provide It with the optimum chances for the experiences It needs. There are karmic implications involved, and this usually means being born into a situation that allows us to relate with others that we are tied to karmicly. The family structure was created partly to serve this need.

Of course, Soul decides as It goes along what It will and won't do within a life. The form and structure of the life is chosen to provide only an opportunity. We may choose not to take advantage of it at that time.

Man is struggling now with the issue of when life begins and ends, and people have died defending their beliefs on this. Until one knows the true workings of Soul, all ideas are based on the principle of the body life. Those working with Soul awareness know that the body will not live more than a few hours without the presence of Soul. When Soul is not present, the machinery of the body begins to stop. Even science's efforts with life support can rarely keep a body going when Soul has departed.

When there is an opportunity for Soul to come to this world It will enter the body of the child generally at the time of birth. It may enter the body a few days before or after birth, but rarely outside these parameters. Before this time the fetus is a part of the female body, and it is always respected that the Soul (mother) inhabiting that female body has the right to decide what It will and will not do as to bringing another Soul into this world.

There is hardly a case where there can only be one life that is best suited for the time. There are infinite variables and we have much flexibility in gathering the needed experiences.

It should be mentioned here that there is a difference between life experience and spiritual experience. Life experiences are the actual events that we go through. Spiritual experiences are the essence of the life experience or the

benefit gained. Soul must learn through spiritual experiences. You can take any given situation that ten people
will be a part of; all of them will realize something a bit different than everyone else, and this can be the spiritual experience gained. It is somewhat deceiving to judge the worth
of a life by the outer appearance of what takes place. Some
people gain little from a seemingly traumatic life experience;
others gain tremendous spiritual insight from the most subtle
moment.

Soul is the only reason these world structures exist. They
are but training grounds for us to find the spiritual meaning
behind the illusions.

13

Vibration

Everything that exists is in a state of action; the atoms of science's discovery are ever in motion, and there are much finer elements of matter that man has yet to discover. This action can be thought of as a vibration, and the measurement of this action is the vibratory rate.

Spirit is the cohesive force that binds the various vibratory rates into harmonious interaction. There is a pulsating effect to action which is seen in Spirit Itself. The energy of Spirit flows outward into the worlds of God, changing Its form of Light and Sound as It passes through the planes of different vibratory bands. Upon passing into the material plane, It returns upward through the planes, reflecting the vibratory rate of each plane again, and on into the depths of the GODHEAD. This cycle is continuous, and the two actions occur simultaneously.

We can see evidence of this action in the tides of the ocean, a pebble dropped in water and the ripples it produces, the revolutions of the planets and the suns, and the very nature of the Lower Worlds with action and reaction.

Every person has their own varying vibratory rate, and it changes with the body, emotional, and mental changes, and Soul's awareness. We can sense another person's vibratory rate and we can see the effect of their rate in what is commonly called the aura, a sometimes multi-colored energy that surrounds the physical and other Lower World bodies. As the rate changes, the colors change; and many conclusions have been made on the meaning of the colors. This study is a subjective one, and it's better to experiment with it yourself than to believe what others have written.

If you have been in a room full of people and suddenly noticed someone enter the room and command attention then you were aware of that person's vibratory rate.

Earth is composed of many elements of vastly different vibratory rates. If a city has large deposits of certain metals in the soil you may or may not feel comfortable living there, as that rate will interact with your own. The oceans have much different rates than the mountains, though both areas are generally found to have less negative influenced rates.

Many people adjust their own rate to better adapt to their environment, and they do this unaware of what exactly has happened. If at all possible, we should find a place to live that feels right for us and surround ourselves with people that we are comfortable with. We should find a study, a city, a mate, and friends that fit us; not the other way around.

Have you ever wondered why some books seem to be written personally to you and others seem to be written in another language? This too is vibration.

You see, the letters we use to form words are symbols for the sound they represent. Words can sound glorious and uplifting, or they can be oppressive and demeaning. The sound interacts with our individual vibratory rate.

When a writer begins to write, he will use his natural pace and rhythm, drawing from the mental and emotional vibratory patterns within himself. The words he uses will reflect this pattern, and your vibratory rate may or may not be compatible with the writer's expression of his vibratory rate.

I introduced a new friend to a very comprehensive book on the spiritual works. She had difficulty reading the lines and reported that the meaning was lost on her. It was obvious that the book was in conflict with her pace of living. After several months of our occasional conversation on spiritual subjects she picked up the book again and had little trouble reading it. Her vibratory rate had risen to a point where she was more in harmony with what was written in the book. This adjustment in vibratory rate was gradual and happened due to a natural progression of awareness and desire. To force an adjustment in rate could lead to serious problems as it will throw the emotions and physical body out of balance.

We know that the words of a rock song are difficult to understand and probably don't make a lot of sense anyway. It's the sound of the song, the pace and rhythm that moves us and gives a message to those who hear it. The message varies depending on how you react to the music. The Sound in music greatly affects the emotional body, whether we react positive or negative, and in high or prolonged doses can affect the other bodies. The vibratory rate of any sound can have an effect on animals as well as humans.

Colors may cause similar reactions in us for they are a reflected form of Light and Sound action. We know that light travels in a wave pattern, and we also know that Light is the companion action to Sound found in Spirit. What is called "coloring," or matching the color of clothes with your body coloring is but harmonizing the vibratory patterns of two reflected objects, the clothes and the body, plus the emotional vibratory rate of the individual, though most will not realize the influence of the rate. They may express it as not "feeling right," but we know what they sense.

Tests were recently conducted on long distance runners, using tinted sunglasses to gauge the endurance of the runner. It was found that certain shades caused the runner to lose energy, while others allowed him to maintain his stamina. It is unusual to find that any covering of the eyes helps in boosting endurance for the body was designed to absorb the normal light around it for energy. We take in the reflected light of the sun for much of our strength. Those who are blind still may benefit from the light, though their body adapts to absorbing the energy through the pores of their skin. People who live for prolonged periods of time in relative darkness will generally have shorter life spans and be troubled with illness.

We commonly react to certain colors in our environment, finding some soothing and others disruptive. Many experiments have been conducted in the workplace to determine the optimum level of efficiency based on the color of the surroundings. If there is a choice it is better that each person suit their own taste in color in an environment that they spend a great deal of time in.

Some forms of healing are centered in adjusting the rate of the body, the emotions, or the mind. Many healers see the aura and make adjustments by gauging the color of the area of trouble. This method of healing can be limited, in that the healer must be able to see the complete extent of the trouble and adjust the cause of the problem instead of the symptoms. There are karmic implications in most forms of physic healing.

The Master is aware of sound when He speaks. It is not unusual to have people tell you that they can't remember exactly what the Master said before a group, but they walked away feeling uplifted. This is because He is able to express an awareness that is from the GOD Worlds, and though the message is filtered by the process of the mind and the spoken voice, it will still carry the essence of the Higher Worlds. This can trigger a point of recognition in those who hear His words, and they are connected again for an instant with that which is close to their own true self, being Soul. The Master's words can be a straight shot to each individual Soul.

The Master can also appear to put people to sleep when he speaks, but usually this is due to His higher rate interacting with Soul, the lower rates of the other bodies are affected in that they are on "automatic pilot" and lulled into nonactivity.

Another point I'll mention is that wherever a Master goes there will usually be some form of turmoil in the outer environment. His vibratory rate will often have uplifting effects, but it can also agitate those who are within a fairly negative band. His rate tends to be very high, though He will adjust it to suit His needs and circumstances. Every Master is channeling primarily the positive aspect of Spirit while occupying a primarily negative body, emotions and mind, not to mention living and working in a negative based world. These forces will tear at each other, and His presence often causes weather changes, unusual behavior in certain people, and can cause failure of electrical devices.

It is wise to remember that the negative force tries in every way to upset the work of the Master, and in this light you can think of Him as being under attack constantly.

If a Master chooses to work in public He will lower His vibratory rate to better harmonize with His surroundings. This allows Him to spend a greater amount of time around other people without completely draining His physical and emotional body, as could happen if He maintained his normally higher rate around the lower rates found in most people. When He is able to be to Himself He will work almost non-stop, perhaps only sleeping for four or five hours a night and be completely rested while in His normal higher vibratory rate.

There are times when it is difficult for my wife to lie next to me. I can be quite comfortable when at times she will experience a burning sensation around her solar plexus, and often will have stomach pains. When I move away she begins to feel better. Even though two people may usually harmonize very well, if one person's vibratory rate is dramatically higher than the other's at that moment the one with the lesser rate can feel physical pain or emotional changes. All of us are able to adjust our rates consciously when we begin to actively work in the spiritual realms.

Adjusting the vibratory rate can be used to keep the physical body warm. There is an old test still given today in parts of the East that involves the spiritual student being wrapped in a wet blanket or robe while sitting in the snow on a rocky cliff in mid-winter. The object is to not only overcome the mental conditioning to being cold but to also raise the vibratory rate so as to warm and dry the wet cloth. I've seen some people melt the snow three feet around them while practicing this. This was once my test and after many attempts I learned to dry the freezing robe. Survival is a good motivation.

When we realize that everything vibrates in its action, then we begin to explore our relationship to all things. This understanding is a tool that can help us to move from being the effect of our environment to being the cause.

14

The
Binding Force

Out of the highest GOD Plane comes a binding force, down through all the worlds of creation, giving directive action and cohesive balance as the voice of GOD ITSELF. Known by many names throughout time, perhaps It is best known as Spirit.

It originates from the highest plane of ITSELF and is the powerful and knowing effect of GOD. This force actually holds the worlds in balance and is the life support for all beings and matter. We may learn of many aspects of IT by working directly with Spirit.

Each plane has a band of vibratory rate, beginning with the Highest Plane. Going down through the other planes the rate decreases in frequency. Spirit has two elements It is most known for, being Light and Sound. It is seen and heard differently on each plane due to the changing vibratory rates. The founders of religions have symbolized It in ceremony, an example being the Catholic Church's lighting of candles and ringing of bells. Symbols for Spirit are found in most faiths, even though the original purpose for their use has virtually been forgotten.

Spirit moves as one force in the Higher Worlds. When entering the Lower Worlds, at the mental plane, It divides into two forces. This separation is known as positive and negative. Once Spirit flows through the worlds to the material plane It then returns upward to the GOD Worlds. This action is constant and we may use this aspect of It to shift awareness to the Higher Worlds.

It was created that the best environment for Soul to gain awareness of Itself and GOD was by having to make knowing decisions. The dual forces of positive and negative give us just that. For every aspect in the Lower Worlds there is an opposite. Good and evil, light and dark, man and woman, left and right, up and down, justice and injustice, to name a few. In choice there is conflict, which leads to growth through experience. This is the play of life.

The dark or negative side we think of is a reality, to be sure. There are beings who are quite capable of ripping the flesh from our bodies and trapping Soul for a seeming eternity. These beings are usually not aware of the big picture; they are carrying out the play of their lives by expressing primarily the negative aspect. Even the rulers of the various planes are seldom fully aware of the Higher Worlds. They too are Soul, and they are subject to the same conditions we face.

The role of the negative is to try to prevent us from discovering who we really are. It is an exacting and intricate process for putting every obstacle in our way, providing you and I with the experiences we need.

The role of the positive aspect is to assist Soul in the discovery. Soul has a choice as to which force It will knowingly channel. While we are in the Lower Worlds we must be part of both forces, but we can choose to actively use one or the other in our basis for living.

Being formed in the Lower Planes; the body, mind, and the emotions have a negative base, while Soul has a positive base being formed from the Soul Plane. Everything born of the Lower Worlds will pass, but Soul is not subject to any limitation, except by Its own awareness.

Our conditioning has developed a fearful attitude about the negative force, but it is wise to remember the purpose of it. We are subject to the negative forces only as we allow, so while we live here in the negative world, we can have our awareness in the positive worlds.

There are causes and effects in the Lower Worlds, laws to

be realized and respected. It can become a game after a while. We know the job of the dark side; we know the purpose of the positive side. When we use our ability to have in our life what we choose, then we are truly free. This balance of forces is known as the middle path.

When Soul balances the lower planes experiences and learns extensively of Itself, It can knowingly find refuge on the Soul plane. There is no need for duality in the Higher Worlds. The conditions we experience in this world are not found in areas of higher awareness. Even after Soul goes to dwell on the Soul plane It will continue to grow into further realization of knowledge and purpose, and there is no limit to spiritual growth. There are no limits to the worlds of GOD; IT is ever expanding and boundless in ITS action.

So we have a choice on this planet. We can choose to manipulate the dark forces to gain the Lower World power for our own use, or we can see the big picture and work knowingly with Spirit to develop our inner abilities so that we may gain a greater awareness of ourselves and GOD. Soul will choose one path or the other based on Its consciousness at the time. Knowingly or unknowingly we make this choice every moment.

There is no right or wrong in the big picture. There is no path that is better or worse for you. There is only the choice that you make for yourself, for this moment. Your choice will carry with it spiritual experiences that are uniquely yours, and every choice will eventually lead you to GOD.

The difference comes in our desire for what we wish to have in our lives. We can play the roles of material life at a slow pace, exploring every facet, and taking the time to grow. Perhaps you are quite comfortable where you are and do not desire to change right now. There is nothing wrong with this, and if it is your choice then I commend you.

You may feel a dim flame inside you that burns with the knowledge that there is another purpose for you besides the Lower World pursuits you've chosen. It may be a small voice deep inside that speaks every now and then, asking you of yourself if you are receiving everything you deserve. You may lie awake one night and not be satisfied with what you have gained so far and know that you have been settling for second best. You have a choice, and you may pursue a path of finding out more about your true self and your true potential.

As in every aspect of the material covered in this book, I could fill volumes with the explanations and methods of Spirit. Perhaps the most important statement to make here however is that Spirit can be a tremendous assistance and comfort while on the path. It is here to provide us with a proven method of gaining awareness, in addition to Its other facets. The positive aspect can be used to bring what we need into reality.

I know many people who feel that Spirit is a friend, and they actively work with It daily. Spirit works in these worlds within a specified framework established by GOD ITSELF. It is capable of bringing into our lives what we need, in a manner that is far superior to what we may do in our limited consciousness.

Yes, this does require faith, but not as you may think of faith. It is more a trust, because when you first give Spirit the opportunity to work for you and see that It can, you will slowly develop a knowing trust that It will continue to work for you. It cannot fail you! Nowhere in the true works are you asked to believe without proof, because you must always prove every element to yourself, no one can give you knowledge. To trust Spirit to bring you what is best for you requires that you test It.

Using Spirit in this way is an accelerated growth. We can plod along using our own abilities, but by asking Spirit to bring into our lives the experiences we need, as we need them, we will speed up the process of realization.

Never do we surrender our will. Soul always has a choice. If we wish to use Spirit, our will simply is that Spirit assist us. We are always free to break away from Its direction or decline an opportunity It provides.

Though far from being mechanical, Spirit does work within certain boundaries, and we can use Its laws reliably time after time. This is open to everyone; if you invoke a law of Spirit, It will return Its appropriate effect. This is also true of the negative aspect of the flow, and we see this in the use of rituals that produce desired metaphysical effects. What few tell you is that there is a price for every action, and it is best if you know what you are buying.

Creative visualization is an aspect of using Spirit to gain what you desire. Basically, you set up a visual and emotional goal within your total self, not just your mind. You must see it, feel it, know it, and also know with unshakable conviction that the goal will be yours. It can be anything that exists. Some people put a picture of their object of desire on the refrigerator so as to better keep the image in their consciousness. One man is said to have done this with a picture of a red Ferrari and within several months he had one. With time you will have your goal, as long as you hold it in your consciousness. This works whether we know of Spirit or not, for spiritual law is action when we use It, regardless of our knowledge of It.

Visualization has been used for thousands of years and is really not a secret. Many groups today have dressed it up and applied other religious angles to it, but there is no need to pay high prices for what is freely yours. Some people call visualization positive thinking, another group calls it a course on miracles, and there is one study that has several large volumes of information with a Christian based foundation. They have lectures and teachers, and the fees can be quite high. The people that I've encountered were concerned with world peace and understanding, and yet they stressed that money was not evil and taught how to have many material objects come into your life.

It is only important that you understand the cause and the effect of this before using it. You will get what you want, be it material or spiritual, but often you may find that you are not as happy with the goal as you thought you would be. Objects have a very limited value and it is so easy to bring into life what we want over what we need. All that we do is not free. Karma does enter into this, as it does most actions.

There is a point on the path when you realize that you want to know more about Spirit, the worlds of GOD, and your true self, and nothing else in this world really interests you anymore. It has never been required that the truth seeker live without material possessions, but rather it is the attachments to the things of this world that slow us down on the spiritual path. You may enjoy your lifestyle, and you can certainly do that and desire to know more. But there is a point where many things here have lost their original value to us, and this point is reached naturally and in perfect balance with our consciousness. It is here that we may begin to rely more on Spirit to bring into our lives what we need in order to best grow.

Not only will Spirit fulfill our desire for opportunity of knowledge, It will use us as channels for Its work if we desire. While Spirit has power to do all things, It relies on Soul to channel the positive flow to accomplish part of Its work. Many people are healed or blessed, events changed, and Souls moved by Spirit working directly through the willing channel of one of us. Often we are not aware of It working through us, but from time to time we can see the miracles, and we know that it was not us personally, but Spirit that performed them.

First we must ask. So many have been discouraged when their lives seem empty, but they must ask in order to receive. The gifts of GOD have already been given in the form of IT providing Spirit for our blessings. We have only to establish a personal relationship with Spirit and ask for It to bring into our lives what we need. Spirit is available to each of us and always has been; we only need to be aware of the fact to work actively with It. After experiencing this firsthand we will trust It to bring us what we never could have provided or imagined. But being an exacting energy, Spirit must be directed by your request, your action, in order to set the process in motion. The effect will be what you desire.

The highest form of using Spirit here, and certainly the path of most reward, is when we commit ourselves to work in GOD's action, and allow Spirit to use us as part of Its will. This is an advanced position, and people may have trouble with it because they are not ready to do this. When you are ready you will know it, and you will willingly work to this extent with Spirit. In being a knowing, full-time channel for

Spirit you understand that your every need will be taken care of, and the road Spirit chooses for you will be the best for the whole picture.

Everything we do has an effect on the worlds about us, and Spirit works to provide the best situations for all concerned when we use It. It is a balance of our energy and Spirit. To give an example, if you were out of work and desired a new position you would ask Spirit to provide the opportunity that benefited the whole. You must also make the effort to answer job ads, go on interviews, talk to people, and in every way help the material process. You will gain many experiences in this participation, and the result will be that you grew in realization while Spirit assisted in getting you the right job.

Here I must mention the difference between what we need and what we want. We can use creative visualization to get what we want, and it may not be at all what we need. We can work directly with Spirit to get what we need, and we will receive the experiences that allow us to gain spiritual realization. Sometimes we cannot see this because times may be discouraging and hard, but in growth there are both pleasurable and painful experiences. It is important that we know this, and decide what means the most to us.

Spirit will never give us what we cannot handle; it is spiritual law that governs this. We can have nothing except in accordance with our state of consciousness, though it may seem that we cannot handle the experience. At times we may think we are on overload when we do not regulate the flow within us. We can channel a flow that is too great for our present awareness and we will feel like we are on fire. Work and family will be strained, and little else will matter but Spirit. Clearly we are out of balance.

I met a man who had this experience in extreme levels. He had practiced a conservative Christian faith until visiting a church that believed in channeling Spirit (they call It the Holy Ghost), speaking in tongues, and laying on of hands for healing. This is a metaphysical study though I know that following would probably not call it that.

This gentleman was moved by what he witnessed in the

church and was open to that energy. The force of Spirit in these circumstances can be great and will be absorbed by many who do not know how to control It. He was completely overwhelmed in the experience and spent many months in turmoil.

He felt as though his body was on fire, he had visions, and he quoted scripture almost non-stop. With time he balanced most of this energy, though it has been a profound time for him, and he will likely remain a channel for Spirit.

It is far better to take the flow of Spirit in gradual doses, to allow your Master to help you to open your awareness to Its ways. This allows time and experience to adjust the vibratory rates of the emotions, mind and body to the new level you will be operating on.

Once you are an active channel for Spirit you may find difficulty if you attempt to block the flow. We cannot hold Spirit within us; we must allow It to work through us in some form.

So how do you establish a personal relationship with Spirit? By being aware of It. By taking a walk along your favorite trail, or sitting and watching the sun set, and being honest about yourself and what you want. Spirit is as close as your own breath, and if not for It none of us could be in this world. It knows you; It has an incredible love for Soul that is not known by human standards because It is spiritual love that It gives direct from GOD ITSELF. Spirit has been aware of you for all time, but in respect for your freedom of choice It must have your request in order to work more directly with you.

The prayers of billions of Souls throughout time have been heard and answered by Spirit for this is the role It serves as the voice and hand of GOD. If your prayers have not been answered, then you have not followed the exacting principles of Its actions. If you are asking for GOD's will to be done, then you must respect the regard Spirit shows for the whole picture.

Spirit will provide you with the information you need, perhaps in the form of a Teacher in your dreams, or in person, a book, or the conversation overheard on an otherwise boring trip home on the train. It will provide you the experience itself by guiding you into situations. You then have the opportunity to combine this for knowledge.

But first you have to ask for Its assistance, and then you must be willing to let It work with you and through you for the benefit of the whole.

It can be your closest friend while here in the Lower Worlds.

To you, wherever you see yourself being, I say this: make a knowing decision for your life.

15
Time

I remember well the Saturday morning in early summer. A few minutes after opening the office, I was sitting behind the counter. The streets were quiet, as were the phones, and the strong smell of coffee filled my mind with distant memories.

The lush green trees moved slowly with the breeze and all audible, hidden life sang in the thick kudzu vines. I was lost in another quiet morning, seventeen years earlier on my grandfather's small farm. He was laughing softly to himself, and I was a boy with no desire to be anywhere else than with him, for all time.

In an instant I was back in the present, and for a split second it occurred to me. No. It can't be that simple. I did it again, and I was amazed. I had stopped time.

Sitting on a wobbly stool, staring at the green brush through the window, it suddenly struck me that I was alive that very second. I drew all my awareness to that exact second in time, and sensed everything I was and could be! There was no awareness of past moments or future, just the world I was experiencing that very second, which was made up of everything I had ever known before. The normal stream of life's moments were brought to a screeching halt and I realized only that moment I was in.

We are not taught to do this. Our human social structure

has been based, in the East and the West, on concepts of past, present and future. They intermingle with each other constantly, and we are caught in a continuum of time. Almost every activity is based on a past or future event, and our present moment is left deciding the implications. Seldom do we block past and future out and see ourselves only in the present second. Doing this may astound you!

Groups of people have been discovered living in remote locations in Central America and the Amazon who have no working concept of past or future. To them there is no time! There is only the moment. Yes, they have memories, but they are viewed in the present context as a reality in this moment. The future is not a factor to them; it is not a concept in their minds.

Here we hint at the truth of time. It lies in our minds and has been established firmly in our social training to such an extent that we do not question it. Time is real only in the mind, and the agreement of many have established it as a universal reality. Time only exists in the Lower Worlds, and it is present in some form on every plane from the mental worlds to the material awareness. But what is time?

Time is the measure of movement from point to point. It is a tool we use here to measure movement, in this planet's case, the movement of the earth around the sun. Time is a necessary tool for man to be organized, and it is a reference gauge to concepts of past and future. Our socially organized world would not function well at all without time, and it is destined to be with us as long as there are the Lower Worlds. Terminology will change, references will shift, but time will remain a tool.

Few people see time as this, however. It is such a strong consideration in our lives that we have made it an integral part of ourselves. The concepts of past and future rule us.

There is much to be learned by reviewing the actions of our past in this life and in past lives. We may be able to better understand the reasons for our decisions. It is when we dwell primarily in the past that we lose control over the present moment. The past is gone. We cannot change those events; we can only view them on the past time track, and perhaps gain awareness that will help us now. Worrying about our past, or the past of someone else, is one of the most common traps we fall into.

The future should be thought of because each moment will unfold into the next moment, and these compounded will become the future. Our actions now will affect those moments, and it is wise to realize the implications of our actions now. The moment now affects the future.

Both directions, past and future, revolve around the present moment, *now*. We can see that this second is the only thing we have control over. We cannot change the past, and the future is not yet here. All we have is *now*.

I stress this because in the Higher Worlds there is no movement, there is no time, there is no space, there is only *now*. If we are to realize ourselves as Soul, and wish to dwell in Soul awareness, or plane, then we must take the first steps by learning how to see the subtle differences of these concepts. Our lives will go on much as before, but at will we will be able to stop time, and be all that we are this very moment. This is the beginning step to self realization, the understanding of the need to have a *knowing* control over each moment.

This control, once understood and practiced, builds on itself so that we do not have to consciously think of it at all. We knowingly *act, right now,* and we understand the effect that action will produce.

We do not have to be slaves to the concepts of time, it never has to rule our lives. Even the busy executive could immediately relieve stress if he stopped for one moment . . . and established the reality of the true self and the present conditions, in that one moment, *right now.*

Try this exercise: Sit comfortably in a chair and stop all movement of your body. Now block any images of things you have to do in the next few moments. Cancel the images of your actions over the last few minutes, and focus your attention on the one material object that is right in front of your field of vision. You are looking at that object right now. This is all that is happening in this very moment; you are sitting down and looking at just the one object when you realize that your life, right now, is in full awareness before you. You have stopped time; you have isolated the moment.

If this does not work for you right away keep practicing, it will work.

Now is all we have control over.

16

Karma

In writing about karma I could fill volumes with the mechanical workings of this study. I could also explain it in several sentences. The reality of karma and the implications of it as it affects our lives is a deceivingly simple concept. Far too much attention is placed on needing to know the karmic balance at hand in a person's life, so much so that it blinds the person from realizing their full potential as Soul.

Attitude is one of the most important aspects in understanding how to travel and gain knowledge in the worlds of GOD. Soul does not exist by rules or methods; It lives only by what It *knows*. If It *knows* how to be in the middle path, It will go through Its experiences with an openness and receptiveness. If It tries to conform to rigid beliefs and rules established to satisfy the mind and emotions, It will meet with confusion and unhappiness. Attitude is the view of life through the senses of the emotions, mind, and increasingly, Soul. The attitude of one on the spiritual path should be one of balancing the mind and emotions to view life from the primary vision and *knowing* of Soul.

While the mechanical function of karma is a basic tool in allowing us to experience, it is also one of the most misunderstood aspects of the spiritual study.

Karma has been written of for centuries, and today people generally think of it as a negative action. It is not. This misunderstanding can trap Soul by involving It in seemingly endless calculations of debt and payment. The more aware Soul becomes of Its past, the more trapped It can become if It tries to track and calculate karma. We use the phrases "bad karma" and "that's your negative karma" to explain many events in our lives that have nothing to do with a negative aspect. The only negative aspect of karma is our attitude of it.

Every action has a reaction in the Lower Worlds; every cause will produce an effect. This is the structure of karma, and it exists so that Soul has the opportunity to choose the course It will take. It is an exacting law, and no one escapes the reality of it, not even the Master. The Master knows how to work within the framework of karma, and He also knows how to work beyond the confines of karma.

Each thought, emotion, and movement is an action, so these will have a reaction somewhere in the realm of the Lower Worlds. Karma is not positive or negative, because it is both and it is neither. You see, every principle is a paradox when viewed in the material senses. Karma simply exists to give us the opportunities to experience, and through this we will gain spiritual awareness. There is nothing to fear or anticipate when we understand this.

Our past actions and reactions will come into balance at some point of our awareness, whether in this life or in lifetimes to come. The relationships with others in our lives are largely involved with karmic settlements. Realizing this can help to explain the moment to moment interactions with those in our lives, and help us to balance them. Sometimes people feel compelled to stay in a relationship because they believe that they must in order to fulfill the responsibilities to another person, or karmic debts. You can only judge the situation at hand to see your place in it, but sometimes the way to balance the obligation is to remove your participation from it, and then balance the load in another way. Staying in a destructive relationship can create more obligation than it satisfies. Karmic debts to others can be resolved in other ways, and in other times. It is important to have as much control, balance, and happiness in your life as you can, in each moment. While you know that you cannot avoid the debt involved, you can often choose the time and method of payment. Make each moment as fulfilling as possible.

Though it is difficult to explain in words, you will know when your karmic responsibilities are settled with someone. There will no longer be a pull or attachment to the person or even to the thought or emotion of that person. Balancing karma in relationships is best handled by practicing personal responsibility as outlined in a previous chapter.

The effects of karma are not always readily seen and may take a long time to express themselves in your life. Some actions can be effected into future lifetimes. Karma is the balancing force that concerns spiritual experiences, not physical experiences alone. What we initiate in a deed may appear as effect in a form that does not resemble the original action. Because I send a charity a hundred dollars today does not mean that I will necessarily receive a hundred dollars from some unexpected source. Rather it is the spiritual act of compassion in giving that will be rewarded in some like form somewhere in the future, in the essence of the act itself.

There are two basic forms of karma studied, being primal and secondary. Primal karma is the long-term karma acquired over the many lifetimes. Secondary karma is the moment to moment karma that takes place with each action. Secondary karma can certainly build into primal karma if not balanced.

Everyone is subject to karma, even the Master. In order to reach Mastership primal karma must be balanced, and to maintain Mastership the moment to moment aspects of secondary karma must be balanced. In order to raise one's vibratory rate primal karma must reach a more balanced level. Vibratory rate and karma are interrelated, in that one will be the effect of the other. Those who have a high vibratory rate will find that the reactive nature of an action will take place more swiftly, and the secondary karma is dealt with in a faster process.

The one way to avoid karma is to act in the full expression of GOD, to be an active channel for GOD ITSELF in the expressed task at hand. The deed is done in the power and action of GOD ITSELF, as IT directs, by an agent of GOD, therefore sidestepping the boundaries of karma. This is how the Master avoids karma; otherwise He must constantly balance His secondary karmic responsibilities. If the balance is lost to a great debt side, then the vibratory rate is affected and this can hinder the freedom of His actions. This rarely happens.

Sometimes a Master will accept a part of a karmic load a person carries, though this is an act of love and compassion that will help the person but not rob the individual of the needed experience the karma may have provided. The Master may carry this load for a short while, perhaps suffering the effect of the karma, and then allow it to be absorbed in the life stream of Spirit.

It is normal to be concerned that our actions of the past may still await payment. It can become a worry and hang over us like a black cloud. This worry and concern is an action in itself and will create more tension, as well as keep us from being all we can be each moment.

Instead of trying to judge our place with karmic responsibilities and attempt to keep score, we would be better served by relaxing and knowing that we are Soul. Everything we have experienced has brought us to where we are today, and we only have control over this very moment, right *now*.

Live your life as best you can, in your natural relaxed manner, by simply being yourself. Your karma will balance itself with time and experience, and each moment you will be greater in your awareness.

Attitude. See yourself each moment, and be all that you can *be*, right *now*. It is that simple.

17

The Ways
of the Master

Every spiritual and metaphysical study has its leaders who have earned some degree of mastery of that subject. We can gain much information by working with these people, and they serve a valuable purpose in the progressive development of Soul's awareness. Whatever we choose to pursue we are wise to remember that there are limitations to every aspect, and it is only by working with someone who has a broader understanding of the big picture that we can gain self realization. There is an emotional phenomena that occurs on the astral plane that can lead us to believe we have gained self realization and a seeming knowingness that occurs on the mental plane, but these are quite different from Soul recognizing itself in Its true environment of the Soul plane. True self realization is Soul realization.

There are many studies that, in truth, have no greater working knowledge than the astral plane and its laws. The followers of each study believe their work to be much higher and have convinced millions that it is the complete path to follow. For those people it will be another experience, and that is part of the play of life. There are works that involve parts of the causal and mental planes, and they too suggest that theirs is the one way to follow. These are experiences, and in themselves are no harm to those that follow them. It is but part of Soul's experience, and all of us are or have been a

111

part of these studies at one time or another. They brought us to where we are right now and provided a foundation for greater realization. This is true of all religious, philosophical, occult and metaphysical teachings.

The information in this book is part of a higher knowledge that comes from experiencing a higher reality. This way is not the only way, but is a suggestion for you to consider, that there is much greater spiritual understanding present on this planet than you may have believed. A Master of this information has worked through the varied teachings on this planet and many other worlds, including the GOD Worlds. There is a process Soul undergoes which we may call Mastership, though few understand it.

As there are various levels of understanding, there are various levels of mastership. The Highest Masters working with those in the Lower Worlds have completed the training of thousands of years of experiences in the bodies. They have studied and mastered virtually every path in its essence. They have a working ability on the Soul plane and have investigated the GOD Worlds. They have been in the presence of GOD ITSELF and learned of ITS secrets and methods. They have been asked what role they would serve for GOD and have willingly chosen to return to the Lower Worlds to work directly with each other and Spirit to aid in bringing information to those who are ready to receive it. These are the Masters I speak of in this book.

Let's think about that for a few minutes. Can such a Being really exist? I have worked with and known many of them, and I have proven their existence and experience to myself by the only true method available.

Throughout time there has been this level of Mastership on this planet. GOD ITSELF directs *One* Master to be the primary channel for Spirit to work through, and this Master assists in this way until handing the position to another. This is part of the order of the worlds, that the positive aspect of Spirit is anchored through one primary channel at the end of the spiritual worlds, the material plane, and then Spirit can be channeled through other Souls.

Various other Masters have work that brings them here,

and it usually concerns teaching those who are ready for the Higher works. In every aspect these Masters are working for the purpose of Soul returning to Its true home. They work in complete harmony with the *One* who is the primary channel, and with Spirit. They have put their will as the will of GOD ITSELF, and they answer only to IT.

All the Masters of this highest understanding teach the same message, that being the true nature of Soul and the worlds of GOD. They may use different words and descriptions, but the basic teaching they give is the same. They have worked with small followings over the many centuries on this planet and passed this knowledge to them in secrecy.

In recent years, a Master who served as *One* who was a primary channel for Spirit was directed to bring these teachings out in the open by speaking publicly and writing dozens of books. It was this Master that one of my Teachers told me of, and I went on to discover His writings and work with Him. His name is Paul Twitchell and His physical work on this planet ended in 1971, and another Master took His place as the *One.* This line of Masters is unbroken in time and can be traced to the dawn of creation of the Lower Worlds.

The teachings of these Masters center on helping Soul to see the illusions that lie in the structures of this world. They teach that Soul can step away from the physical body, as well as the astral, causal and mental body, and know Itself and the worlds of GOD.

The fear of death is eliminated by Soul leaving Its body at Its own will and then being able to return any time It chooses. One day It will give up this clumsy human shell in death, but the experience will be little more than It has experienced by leaving the body. When I speak of leaving the body I am talking in physical senses. All we really do is shift our awareness to but another point within us. We come into agreement or harmonize with the vibratory band found in the reality we wish to observe and participate in.

All the worlds of GOD lie within us, not outside of ourselves. We have only to *be,* right *now,* and we are stopping the illusion of time and space and living in the ever present *now.* At this point we direct our attention to another facet or world within us. We can knowingly work with the Masters and others on any plane we have the ability to *be* with.

One problem people have in "leaving their body" is that they think of themselves moving outside of their body and experience. There is nothing outside of us but the atmosphere of the material world. The Reality lies within us; we have only to come into agreement with or shift our focus and attention to another point.

Just as we can think of "leaving the body" as being outside of ourselves, we often think of the Master as being beyond anything we can have for ourselves. In fact, with the help of a Master we can become the Master of our world and work knowingly alongside one of these spiritual giants. We, too, will one day become a Master.

Of course, the Masters teach by giving us this information. They cannot do it for us; they only point the way. The lives and workings of the Masters are understood little, even by those that claim to follow them, largely because they are judged by material and social standards, and many see them through their own emotions and minds. Part of gaining a higher realization is becoming aware of how these spiritual Beings become the Master.

Before attaining Mastership, He has studied extensively in the previous lives before entering the body of a child in this world. He has most probably attained self realization in a previous life, but not necessarily. He grows up like many around Him, except that He is worked with closely on the inner planes by a series of Teachers or Masters. He has a choice and can at any time step away from the work. He has to undergo many of the physical ordeals that others do, and He must come into conscious realization of Himself as Soul and His abilities before he can claim His place of Mastership.

By working with a Master he learns of the GOD worlds, and eventually He is able to travel there on His own. Even though He has been in the presence of GOD He is not yet the Master. The other Masters will work with Him and refine His abilities before He steps fully into that position. In several cases that I have known it was anywhere from four to eight years after gaining GOD awareness before Soul developed fully into the Mastership. Though this moment is *known* within to the individual, it is a subtle realization. For all the mental structure we place on the process of realization and the areas of attainment, it is but another step and another moment in the awareness of Soul. He has learned to live in the *now* and is humbly aware that He does not hold all knowledge. The journey into GOD awareness does not end. Yet He is now ready to assist those who ask for guidance on the spiritual path.

With the awareness of GOD ITSELF He will decide His role for IT, and this is usually according to the needs of the Order of Masters. This is an informal, yet powerful, group of those who have attained Mastership, and who work in harmony with each other for the advancement of all Souls.

The Master who is chosen by GOD to be the *One* who primarily channels Spirit comes into this world in much the same way, except that He may have attained Mastership previous to being born here again. If this is the case, He has willingly chosen to be reborn in a physical body and accept the work of becoming the *One*. A Master's karma is completely balanced, and He does not have to continue the cycle of life and death unless He wishes. This is a tremendous responsibility, and few have an idea of the burden it can carry. The Master performs His duty with only one purpose, and that is to serve GOD in whatever way IT desires.

Sometimes this *One* makes known His position, but history shows that most have worked with a relative few outwardly. Man seeks to protect the structures formed in religions, and persecution has been common. It has also been that only a few were ready to hear what the Master teaches. It is not that the truth of GOD is a secret, but rather that man has not desired or seen the truth when put before him. This, too, is the play of life and is in balance with the spiritual unfolding of Soul.

Today the chosen *One* is known and often appears before the public to discuss the fundamental teachings. He supports the outer organization that was established some twenty years ago, which acts as a cohesive distribution point for the writings now published. The teachings and methods of this organization are an excellent way for the new seeker of higher truth to begin the active path, and I recommend it highly. There comes a point with this teaching, as it is with all outer teachings, when the seeker will leave it to learn primarily on the inner planes. We must find GOD alone. It is only that we have outgrown the need for the organized study and methods. This is the flow of life.

I have known many Masters who live completely unknown to the masses. They may work a job with no outer sign of being different and in the body they aren't. They mingle with the people they meet daily and also work with others on the inner planes. They have chosen an area of spiritual work that calls for this manner of living, and they are not discovered unless they wish to be.

There are those who live in the hills and mountains and rarely have human contact, though they are very active in the inner reality. Each plane has its Masters who assist both the Soul living on that plane and those who visit seeking knowledge.

When you request assistance from Spirit, It knows your position and awareness and may link you directly with one of these Masters. The Master uses Spirit to a great degree, and is freed of many petitions and requests that Spirit may handle directly. Once you come under the watchful eye of a spiritual Master He will always be close to you, though you may not be aware of it. He has many ways of assisting you and will usually use methods that allow you to determine your own success. Rarely is anything handed to you.

While using a human body the Master is subject to the laws of the material plane, as well as the astral, causal, and mental planes. He has emotions and a mind that He must keep in balance. Many may think of a Master as a state of perfection, but this is not so. In Soul awareness He has attained GOD consciousness and has many abilities over the conditions of the countless planes. But perfection is a mental concept and has never existed except in the minds of men. What we seek is balance, not perfection, of all of our bodies.

There is a range of action in balance, and it allows for small excesses in both directions, as well as the center position. For example, in the emotions you may see a Master laugh loudly, be completely neutral in expression, or show some signs of sadness. This is the likely range of emotional expression found in Mastership. Rarely will you see anger, depression, or uncontrollable happiness, unless He has a reason to display these feelings. There may be an experience that someone needs at that time, and though He risks being misunderstood by others who witness this, He will give of Himself to help the Soul in His charge.

You can think of balance as centering a pencil on the tip of your finger. With little effort you can cause the pencil to tilt to one side and then the other without allowing it to fall off. This is much like the balancing act we do with our mind, emotions and body. If the pencil falls off you're out of balance, but a Master does not allow this to happen in His life.

A Master is not very concerned with appearances or material goods. He needs money to live just like everyone else, but He is not attached to things of this world.

The Master may marry and raise children. He may do anything that you may do, because He is in this world. It is foolish to judge the outer life He lives, though He is aware that He is judged. The Master works only for the good of the whole, never selfishly, but in this may easily be misunderstood. His judgement is not to be challenged, though you must personally decide for yourself the meaning of His actions as they affect you. Those that try to harm a Master, whether they know He is one or not, will encounter great difficulty. The Master does not strike back but rather the offensive action is reflected by the positive energy of Spirit the Master holds, and the aggressor is faced with his own action returning to him.

He can heal; He can work miracles, but will seldom do this in a way that will call attention to Him. He humbly will tell you that He is but a channel and co-worker with GOD, and He of Himself did not do the deed. Almost every action He takes is in the name of GOD and for ITS purpose, not His own. In this He avoids the cycle of karma, for it is only by living in the action of GOD that it can be avoided. The few acts that involve secondary karma are balanced almost immediately so as not to compromise His awareness.

The Master is Soul who has attained that position, but will be the first to tell you to never worship Him or any other Soul. Never follow anyone for a Master will not lead you. He will point the way with utmost respect for you and will stand back and allow you to choose your path. He will show you how to work with Spirit, and how to master the worlds on your own. He will show you that there is not a right or wrong way, that there is only difference and the middle path.

The Master will show the attitude of unattachment and how to see the middle path in all things.

He will rarely tell you His position openly when asked, He will instead tell you to go within and find the answer. And then to trust the answer. When commanded to reveal His identity, He will gaze into your eyes and tell you His truth deep within your being. You will know who He is, though He may never say a word.

The Master gives spiritual love and good will to all and will not be involved in disputes that center on right or wrong. He gives you your choice. While He is concerned with each Soul, He is working for the good of the whole as it impacts on the work of GOD.

He may stand beside you in the grocery store, and you may not know Him because you are looking for someone who fits the worldly concept of a Master. He is a spiritual giant in a human body. He is here to break the molds that hold you prisoner; He is involved in your life only because you asked Him to be.

There are thousands of people on this Earth who can heal or destroy, who can see the future or the past, who can know or influence your thoughts. There are ten thousand more who can sway the crowds with emotional control, leading the multitudes to a supposed happier life. How do we judge these people?

All the metaphysical skills, and they are skills, are performed by learning and practice. The Lower Worlds are made up of specific laws that govern the balance of material matter. Metaphysics is simply the applied action of some of those laws; they will serve anyone if applied correctly. Natural science is but another area of these laws; these are the ones that have found common acceptance. These laws exist whether we are aware of them or not, and they can play a major role in our understanding of ourselves. And yet mastering the laws of the Lower Worlds will not in themselves get us closer to GOD.

The miracles of the Master are Lower World acts of GOD, performed as the will of GOD. It is a common misconception to think that a Master can perform any metaphysical act that He wants. The road to Mastership has us experiencing many different studies and actions, and most everyone will go through the major groups of study before attaining Mastership. Generally a Master comes into this world in His last necessary incarnation, having walked down all those roads before. In this life He will come to realize what lies beyond the influence of the Lower Worlds, and while everyone will retain select areas of ability, as this is the personal nature of each of us, attaining Mastership is dicovering that GOD lies in the essence of all of IT.

For example, available to everyone is the ability to tap into the Soul awareness within themselves, where they can know whatever they choose. There is a definite process of shifting awareness that most everyone goes through, no matter how proficient they are at it. It is a rapid step-by-step technique of shifting awareness, usually using visualization. A Master does not need to do this; He just *knows*. There is an instant line of awareness open, although the Master does not walk around constantly with GOD awareness. The Master balances awareness within Him to adjust instantly to the moment at hand.

Another example is healing. The physical and emotional body can be healed by using metaphysical methods. These are prayers, laying on of hands, positive thinking, visualization, chants (vibratory action), and various combinations of these. They all have the same effect, and that is a limited action caused by another. The healing is often temporary and most certainly carries a karmic implication. But it makes for good show and millions have followed and supported those who heal. The Master will rarely heal another. The Master is a channel for Spirit, that is one of His roles here, to work closely with Spirit in a joint effort for the work of GOD. Spirit may remove the burden of an illness from someone, and the Master may channel this energy, but it is rarely the desire of the Master Himself. He sees the bigger picture, realizing that in illness and suffering there are the lessons of life. There are often karmic balances in motion, and these are essential for Soul to mature. When the Master does work with Spirit in healing it is often on the inner planes and rarely publicly.

The point is that parlor tricks don't make a Master. The Master may or may not have the technical Lower World skill to walk on water, but you can be assured that if He needs to he will! The work of GOD will not be delayed by a small technicality.

The Power a true Master holds is a reflection of the Power of GOD, and the Master claims no power of His own. The same is true of the Love of the Master; it is a reflection of the Love of GOD, and He channels this energy and aware- ness on behalf of the work that has brought Him here to this planet. Though few will understand this statement, it is true that a Master is the representation of GOD in this world.

It is often the goal of the seeker to have the Master visit him in the spiritual body and share great wisdom. After all, some people have said that they had this experience, and it has been written about extensively. Why doesn't this happen for everyone?

The Master does work with every sincere seeker, and much of this occurs in the dream state. At first you may not remember these sessions; you may only know that you un- covered something in the distant mist of your being. With time and spiritual experience you will begin to bring more and more information back with you, until you will eventual- ly have total recall. The Master works in the dream state because we are at first more receptive then, free of many of the emotional and mental blocks that may stand in the way.

You may feel a need to have proof of the Master being in your life, and in fact, the Master asks that you prove all of it for yourself. We may mistakenly look for physical proof, and while there are physical effects of growing on the path, the proof lies largely within us. The Master points out that too often we look outside of ourselves for answers. We may think that a certain knowingness is beyond us, and it always will be if we believe that. All of reality lies within our own perceptions of the world that we are unto ourselves. Nothing is outside of us, everything is within!

From time to time a Master may appear in a physical body to work with someone, and this is usually because that person has a strong need to have the mind satisfied. The mind must rationalize the existence of everything, and much of the higher studies is an effort to undo previous concepts and accept new ones. The emotions are another factor that the Master must help the seeker to balance.

Usually when someone speaks of a Master visiting them it is actually the seeker tuning in to where the Master is, and the discourse is carried out in the spiritual worlds. The Master works with many in the spiritual body.

The Master can be in a human form, with a body, mind and emotions just like us all but He cannot physically be with everyone. The ironic part of this is that those who are around the Master physically usually fail to recognize Him for who He really is.

The most common way the Master works with you is a direct method of using vibratory pulses, Soul to Soul. There are no words spoken, no concepts, no emotions. You may all at once realize a new understanding, whether from the dream state or while awake. The Master directs His Being and Light to the real you, Soul, and gives you the information you need at that time to combine with your experience, and you have a new realization. The mind is bypassed, along with the other lower bodies. In the Soul plane and Higher Worlds we do not use the mind to form images of what we know. We just *know*. There is no movement, no sound as we hear it now, no emotions. The Master knows your needs; He knows your progress. He always gives you what you need at that time, though it may not be recognized because it is not what you wanted.

So many people are looking for spiritual proof in phenomena, and some are satisfied with that. So be it.

Know that the Master works with you in the most intimate way imaginable, Soul to Soul. Look into yourself and see if your personal world is better now than ever before. Are you being challenged and fulfilled personally, living up to all you want to be? You can ask for the Master to be involved in your life, and then He will never leave you.

Your Master may speak directly to you in either the dream or contemplation; you may both see and hear Him or just recognize His voice. Perhaps you just sense His presence in your life. If you doubt the reality of this experience, demand while it is happening that He identify Himself and by spiritual law He must. He will either answer you directly or He may fill your spiritual body with intense warmth and you will *know* it is Him. If you are still left in doubt, demand in the name of GOD that the being or illusion vanish if it is not the Master and draw all the power of your being into the demand. It will leave you if it is not the true Master.

Some people are not comfortable following a Master, and in fact the Master is not comfortable being followed. He would rather be your friend because He is only in your life because you want Him to be. He only suggests ways to solve problems that you have asked help on. The choice is always yours.

Some people contact Spirit and feel guidance there, which is fine. The Master and Spirit work hand in hand, and you may work directly with It. Actually, by turning to Spirit you will find that you are in fact turning more to your own resources. Spirit acts so subtle that you reach deeper into yourself for results. The image of the Master has risks of the seeker becoming dependent, which He does not want. By turning to Spirit, It will slowly teach you to work with your own abilities, combined with the action of Spirit. This can be the normal progression of the teaching, first working with the Master, and then He may turn you over to work directly with Spirit. Of course, He is always close by and watches. The final teaching before gaining Mastership is a long series of work with your Master again, a fine tuning of all you've gained. Then you are a Master and on your own.

18

Initiations

I was eating lunch in the side office; the lights were off in this cramped space of the parts store, and my mind drifted away from work to several areas of thought I had been pursuing. I had been a part of the outer organization for about a year and had many experiences, though most had been very subtle.

When I finished eating, I folded my arms and rested my head on the desk top. While detached, I wasn't asleep when I saw the image of a man walk toward me. I was seeing this in my mind's eye and I followed His movement as if watching a scene in a movie. He was tall and dressed in a hooded robe which outlined His lined, white-bearded face. I was suddenly startled by the reality of His presence and I lifted my head and opened my eyes. Everything was normal around me. When I put my head down again He was there. I looked around me again and made sure I was awake and rational. Deciding I was, I rested my head again and closed my eyes. He was still there and simply stared at me. I watched closely as He bent over, and it was then that I saw a flowing river of light behind Him. He lifted a globe of light in His cupped hands and offered it to me. I was overwhelmed by this gift, and yet my mind did not want to accept what was happening. I could feel the light enter me, going deep within my being, and then I lost awareness.

I awoke and looked around me. Only a few moments had passed on the clock but I had traveled across time and space and was given Light by the Master, though I did not then know His name. My inner awareness was limited and I had seen Him in a black and white scene. Later I was to realize that as we open our consciousness we can not only retain more of the actual experience in our mind but can sense more vividly the color and texture of the plane we are in.

When I practiced the contemplative exercises it was not unusual for me to hear different sounds as I wandered through the different areas of awareness. After contemplating for about twenty minutes during one exercise, I remember thinking that the refrigerator must have come on because I could hear a low, mechanical sound all around me. I opened my eyes and tuned back to the room to find total silence. Sometimes I would hear a faint one-note sound of a flute, and other times I heard rushing water. The different areas of vibratory action can be sensed as sound.

Light and Sound are the two aspects of Spirit found in the worlds of GOD, and on the material plane the evidence is plentiful. The Light and Sound are found in every area of the Lower Worlds and sensed through the awareness we hold. In the Higher Worlds there is no form or being that can be conceptualized as Light or Sound, and yet Spirit does exist and expresses Itself as the Voice of GOD with a presence that is known to the very innermost consciousness. When trying to relate the realization here the closest image to that experience is Light and Sound.

Just as Sound is sensed differently on the various planes, Light appears as various colors as we shift our attention to different areas within the Lower Worlds.

We can raise our own vibratory rate by observing either the Light or Sound while in contemplation and then becoming absorbed in our attention of It.

When a Master appears within and offers either form of Spirit, He is raising your vibratory rate and your awareness potential. This is often called an initiation.

It is normal to feel that there is a gap between what you know inside and what your mind can grasp. How many times have you *known* the answer to a question but could not mentally pinpoint the source of that information? Often we have realizations in dreams and cannot remember them once we awaken. When working with experiences of the Lower Worlds the reasons for this are limited paths of receptiveness in the emotions and in the mind.

Soul is experiencing the event within us, Soul is the real self, and It tries to impress the emotions and the mind with the realization It knows. If we are emotionally afraid of change or new experiences, we have an emotional body that operates at a vibratory rate too low for Soul to make a lasting impression on it. Perhaps there are fear factors that restrict attempts of broadening the awareness. The mind works in patterns, sometimes we call them ruts, and it only recognizes images from sources it is familiar with. If the image is of a higher vibratory rate than the rate of the mental band of awareness, there will be resistance to the image.

When Soul is experiencing the Higher Worlds it is common that the mind and emotions will not hold the experience because the information is beyond the images and vibratory patterns normally recognized.

The Master works with those who are in His charge to help raise the vibratory rate of the emotions and mind and in doing this will raise the total vibratory rate of the individual so that the other bodies will relate to the awareness of Soul. This was the original purpose of the initiation. The term initiation has been used by many groups in metaphysical studies, resulting in many variations and has led to misunderstandings.

There are groups today who will initiate someone upon first beginning a study. The initiation will likely consist of telling the individual that that particular path is the true way to spiritual enlightenment and that once beginning there is no turning back. Devotion is sworn to the teacher. The teacher may then instruct the person in breathing exercises to relax the body and then to chant outwardly a special name of GOD or another spiritual word. The teacher will then give a secret word to the person to use and instruct that the person begin to silently chant the word within. If the teacher has the ability to plant impressions into the emotional and mental body of the person, he will. These impressions are of devotion to the teacher, to the path, and then the image of a sound and a light. The secret word will raise the appropriate vibratory rate and the individual will feel joy and release and sometimes sense a new, often undefined realization. This technique can be used with the first initiation and on advanced initiations, the changing of the secret word being the primary difference.

The danger in this is in using a charged word in inner or outer repetition without the proper spiritual guidance from an experienced teacher. The combination of the rush of new information provided by the teaching and sudden raising of vibratory rate can leave the emotions and mind out of balance and result in many problems.

When a true Master is working with someone He is involved with the inner and the outer reality of the individual. He knows that the best way of attaining spiritual enlightenment is through a more natural balance of information and experience. He will instruct the student with information for a period of time, sometimes as long as three years, before giving an initiation. This allows the mind and emotions to challenge the information in their own environment. The first initiation will probably be on the inner planes, perhaps in a dream, and may take a form similar to my experience with the Master offering me the Light. This first experience will raise the vibratory rate of the mind and emotions and will allow some of the previous information given to connect with previous inner experiences. The goal here is to bridge the different spiritual bodies in harmonious vibratory rates with Soul.

A period of time later, depending on the individual, an outer initiation can take place. This will consist of a session of contemplation where a secret spiritual word is given on the inner planes. The Master then confirms this word outwardly with the individual and offers suggestions as to its proper use. This word is powerful enough to raise the rates of the bodies slightly, but not so powerful as to cause the person to lose balance. Future initiations will involve more highly charged words, suited to the individual's development. There is no oath given to the Master or to the path, because a true Master knows that He is not to be followed and that the path will change with the development of Soul. The Master will point out to the person that once he begins the way to GOD there is really no turning back, as Soul will not be happy until It *knows* GOD.

While an outer initiation does raise the vibratory rate of the physical body, it is more designed to bridge the mental awareness with Soul. Almost every change in rate of the other bodies will affect the rate of the physical body, as they are all interrelated. An outer initiation will have a greater effect, normally, because the outer senses of the mind and emotions are more involved. This helps to bridge the gap between what Soul *knows* and the mind realizes.

Eventually Soul can relate more subtle impressions directly to the mind because the ruts, or bands of receptiveness, are broadened sufficiently to accept the new information as coming from a part of itself. The emotions will be balanced enough over time to contain the range of feelings experienced, providing that fear factors have been dealt with and balanced.

There are structured initiations found in a few studies that are more balanced and require a period of study time before taking an initiation. It is wise to take a careful approach before becoming involved with any group that uses vibratory initiations, the other types of initiations are ceremonial. Take the time to find out who the leader of the group is, what his level of ability is, and then prove his position to yourself. If your teacher is a couple of steps ahead of you in discovering the inner worlds then you are both groping for guidance.

At times we place too much importance on outer initiations. Throughout time there have been those who did not work with an outer Master but did work with Him inwardly. The initiations were inner adjustments and did not take place physically. One can progress on the path in this fashion, though it is better to work with a Master who can give an outer and inner initiation. The progress will be faster and

carries less risk of becoming unbalanced. We carry awareness of our outer world and an increasing awareness of the
inner worlds, so it is necessary that we keep them balanced in
order to work effectively in both.

In many initiations the teacher has the individual bring
fruit to offer as a sign of giving one's self to GOD. This is a
symbolic gesture that reinforces the mental concept of what
is about to take place. Many rituals are used in spiritual
studies to help the mind and emotions accept what is about to
take place. In higher studies there are few rituals, and eventually there are none.

In past eras it was far easier for a Master to work with the
few who looked to Him for guidance. He could closely
monitor each person and give them the information and initiation they needed, when they needed it. While it is true that
all that are on the path have cycles of spiritual development,
we are all different in our approach and understanding of
what is happening to us. The idea that there should be no less
than two years of study between outer initiations is based on
the cycle of development likely to be present for most on the
path, but there are many exceptions in both directions. A few
progress more quickly while most should take more time to
grow.

With so many people actively on an outer path it is impossible for one Master to physically work with everyone, so
He allows those who He has worked with over time, those
who are more advanced, to take the training necessary to initiate others. This can work but always there is the danger of
an overwhelming ego entering into the works.

To assign a rank to an initiation is inviting conflict. There
are groups who do this and others who don't, and they may
even go so far as to teach the danger of ego with the growth.
Whether a rank is given or not, if it is known what level of initiation is given to another there will be those who think that
they are not as far along as that individual, and those who
think that they are farther along. An initiation in itself is not
a sign of spiritual knowledge or place in the spiritual worlds;
it is simply the mechanical balancing of Lower World bodies
with Soul's awareness.

There are those who begin an outer spiritual path with a great resource of inner knowledge, and they have likely been working with a series of Masters over many lifetimes. These people will begin the outer path and initiations much like everyone else because they need to gradually raise the vibratory rates of the mind and emotions in order to connect better with Soul's understanding. There are others on the path that go through many outer initiations and yet have not gained the knowledge in Soul awareness that others might have. Initiation does not in itself signify spiritual awareness, though it is true that one who is allowed to take a more progressed, higher initiation must be able to work in that area and therefore have the conditioning and background to handle the higher vibratory rate.

As an outer study must be somewhat structured to work effectively with groups of people, it is not unusual to have these structures work against the goals when used improperly. As long as we feel competitive and superior to others we are forgetting the purpose of the study and the underlying principles. It is this kind of confusion that causes many to avoid an outer organization.

Soul is equal in spiritual place to every other Soul, even though each individual is in a different area of awareness. There is no one more humble than the spiritual Master because He knows that He is but a small part of the Creation, and only exists by the Love and Power of GOD.

19
Healing

Mankind suffers from many forms of illness on this planet, and on every plane there are some degrees of disharmony with the outer covering, or body. The cause of pain and sickness is on one hand easily explained, and yet on the other it can be very difficult to understand when approaching it from a material viewpoint.

The human body is designed to normally last for a limited, though varied time. While we can provide better diets, supplements, and drugs to fight illness; the body will one day wear out. The only exception is if you learn how to suspend the aging process indefinitely, which has been done for certain purposes by a few Masters. There are those who are said to have spent hundreds of years in the same body.

While we are in the human body we are wise to try to stay in good health and at least pay attention to its basic needs. We need the body to be here, and we are here for many important experiences. To cut this life short through neglect is simply prolonging the time needed in the material world, and we will probably return here to face the lessons that we avoided. Sickness and pain easily fill the consciousness and can distract us on the path.

Karma is not always the primary reason for sickness, though it is true that every action is part of the karmic balance. Sometimes we may choose to take the burden of suffering from someone and carry this load ourselves. The Master may take the illness from one and allow it to be absorbed in the flow of Spirit, or He may carry the illness Himself if the circumstances dictate. The Master knows and understands the workings of karma in this practice.

The factors of being born with certain limitations and developing diseases are largely so that Soul may gain spiritual experience through the physical problems, though this is not always seen in advance. Some people use the catchall concept of handicaps being negative karma in nature, but this is an oversimplification of a complex matter. No matter how the limitation comes about, the result is ultimately the same in the big picture, Soul will gain experience. I am not suggesting that we should not try to advance medicine and other healing methods for these too contribute to the experience of mankind. I am but explaining a cause for man's suffering.

This applies, too, to the starvation found in many countries on this planet and disasters such as drought, hurricanes, and earthquakes. They are the product of an ever-conflicting struggle of negative and positive forces, the very center of this material plane. Souls caught in this struggle will have yet another opportunity to gain spiritual experience, and even if we cure all diseases and prevent all disasters and war, the natural conflict of the two forces will provide for new struggle. This is the way of the Lower Worlds.

Many people spend much of their lives attempting to feed the starving, prevent nuclear wars, and healing the sick. They are not right or wrong in doing this. This is their experience, and perhaps they feel the need to work toward these goals.

The Masters teach that the first spiritual obligation is to ourselves as Soul, for it is only once we truly know the spiritual love of GOD that we can in turn express this love toward others. This is not selfishness, but rather it is the survival of Soul by It coming into awareness of Its position. People who are working for changing the conditions of man are usually not expressing this love, though they may believe that they are. They are caught up in the emotional struggles of the astral plane. This is their experience, and this is in place. It is only important that you be able to recognize the difference if you would attain Mastership.

Emotion plays a large role with this subject. I have met many people who consider themselves devoted to healing the sick, and they often use psychic methods such as mental power, laying on of hands, or direct transfer of energy. They feel their life is for no other purpose than to serve mankind. So be it.

As there is a need in the study of karma, there is a need when we look at healing to try to see the big picture instead of the isolated event. When I was young I worked in the hospital section of a center for retarded children. There I not only saw the most pitiful conditions to afflict children, I cared for them daily. Many times my heart went out to these babies who would be sent there to die. Science had no cure, and the hearts of the parents, the doctors, and the staff were moved with their presence. I've had several babies die in my arms, and I have felt the profound helplessness of human emotional caring with no way to help.

In one instance I challenged a doctor's decision to cease life prolonging efforts. I had grown attached to a child who was slowly dying despite all the actions of the staff. Even though there was nothing science could do, I wanted to maintain every attempt. Later I was to see that the doctor was correct to let the child die in peace. We must see the big picture to escape the illusions of emotion.

I will not pretend to have strict guidelines to follow on healing for it is up to each of us the burden we wish to carry or the viewpoint we will express. Every moment is filled with new and different conditions for us to decide on; there can be no black or white rules to go by. All that is important is that we are aware of the spiritual laws that affect us so that we may make knowing decisions. If we heal through Lower World abilities we will share in the karmic responsibility of the person we heal.

The view of the Master is that man must go through a variety of experiences, and His outlook is involved with that process. While the Master may have the ability to psychically heal any one He chooses, He knows that by doing so He will probably rob that Soul of an experience he is here to receive. The Master can see the karmic patterns in Soul, and He knows what must be. Out of respect for the process of realization of Soul, He will allow It to make Its own choices, no matter the Lower World viewpoint.

There are instances where a Master will heal within the guidelines of Spirit, and the healing is carried out in the inner planes, at the source of the problem. The karma is carried briefly by the Master, and then released within the flow of Spirit. An act of this nature is viewed with a higher understanding of what is needed for that Soul and for the other Souls involved, such as family, and often will enable It to progress more quickly on the path to GOD.

The key difference in spiritual healing is the intent and viewpoint of the one who heals. Are you helping Soul to progress on the path to GOD, or are you robbing It of a much needed experience, and prolonging the spiritual struggle? Very few people know the difference. One question you may ask yourself is whether you are willing to take the responsibility for the action.

Make a knowing decision for your life.

20

The
New Age

The term "New Age" is commonly being used to describe a time from some twenty-five years ago and on into the foreseeable future when a broader understanding of spiritual thought is being brought out into the open. When I pick up an article to read or hear a discussion on television or radio about the New Age, it always seems to center around metaphysical topics. This is an indication of how few people, who are well-versed in Lower World concepts, have little knowledge of the true purpose and home of Soul. I am asked often about the place of these subjects in our daily lives and will offer a few words of observation.

A Short Story

If you were living in Virginia and you heard that the promised land, your true home, was in California, you would start walking in that direction. Along the way you would find many who would not believe there was a promised land and many more who simply didn't care if there was one or not.

You may recognize that an automobile would be a useful device to get you there, and you would find that there was an amazing interest by many in how the automobile worked. So much so that they take it apart and rearrange it, often using its parts for other purposes than transporting the body over distance. Countless books are written on the basic science of how the integral parts make the car run, and many studies are formed on how the internal combustion engine operates. This is perceived to be a higher study and can consume the lifetimes of thousands around you, though no one has anywhere to go with this information.

You are left wondering why no one else wants to get in the car and drive to California.

Channeling

A popular topic now is channeling, and to understand this you must first determine what particular energy is being channeled. There are three basic areas to draw from—being Soul awareness, channeling Spirit directly, or channeling an entity's presence from another plane.

Many people relate that they are channeling from their "higher self" and I take this to mean their Soul awareness, though they could be, at times, channeling Spirit. All of us can do this. From what many of these people are saying they must believe that their higher self is outside of their normal awareness, and this is a perception that limits us from being all we can be. Soul is always trying to make Its will known to the mind, and we can use Soul awareness most of the time when we learn the difference between the mind, emotions, and Soul.

Some people claim to channel the will or Spirit of GOD and they use this most often in healing and prophesy. They may be channeling Spirit, but you must judge the implications of this for yourself. It is wise to remember that Spirit has two aspects working in the Lower Worlds, both positive and negative. The underlying methods of tapping into Spirit are the same regardless of the aspect channeled, so if a negative power is used to heal someone the act will carry the effect and responsibility of the action. Healing, in itself, is not a positive action. Rarely would we think of sticking pins in a voodoo doll as being a divine expression of Spirit, and yet this mock-up is used in rituals that do cause a desired effect, all within the negative aspect of Spirit. Most people who claim to channel Spirit are full of good intentions and do not have complete awareness of the duality of this power.

The last area is channeling an entity or Soul from another realm of awareness, which is similar to what a medium would do. I have not seen this to be of much value and have rarely seen it to be actually happening. A Soul from another plane can be met and talked to directly by shifting your awareness to where It is at, so why use a medium when you can do it yourself? In allowing someone else to be the go-between you risk the medium bringing their own subjective viewpoint into the discussion. Most people who can channel this energy do not have the ability to deal directly with the entity, rather they hear and feel impressions. The truth is that most people who claim to be able to do this are hearing the voice of their own mind, not the voice of an entity.

In fact there is little to be learned from most Souls in other realms, and when we contact them it is much like talking to a stranger on the street. Sometimes you can petition for a spiritual contact and if your astral senses have enough desire you will attract an astral entity who will draw upon your energy for their own fulfillment. This can lead to an attachment that can be difficult to break.

It is extremely unlikely that a Master working from another realm would work through a medium, as there is simply no need for this. A Master would not normally work through another person for your benefit. You are responsible for initiating contact with the Teacher, and He will work directly with you. If the entity contacted does not have the ability to work directly with you in either the waking or the dream state I would continue to search for the Master. Otherwise you could be dealing with a very limited power and the chances for wrong information are very high.

Crystals

Crystals are popular now and many claim that they bring a special energy to their lives. A similar claim is made about the shape of the pyramid. There is a basis for fact in some of these claims in that energy can be altered when used in certain conditions with these objects. This has been known for thousands of years and has been used on all parts of the planet. I was in a large bookstore a few weeks ago and saw a crystal kit, complete with instructions and several badly cut stones placed behind a plastic wrapping. This doesn't take anything away from the reality of crystals, but it does indicate the new level of popularity of metaphysical topics. The manufacturer brought them out just in time for Christmas sales.

What I have seen happen more often than not is an amazing amount of attention being placed on these objects, and a belief that they can make one's life better. A strong belief can do a lot to change one's life and this is seen by the wearing of the cross by Christians or another emblem that represents a strong force in us. A good luck charm such as a four leaf clover or rabbit's foot can do the same thing for someone who believes in it. The voodoo doll and pins have power over some people. The power is in the belief, not the object. In themselves crystals will do little to help us to *know* GOD.

Astral Projection

Astral projection is the subject of dozens of books and yet is is largely misunderstood. When we focus on the astral body or awareness and make an effort to separate it from the awareness of the other bodies, we will be aware of only the astral senses. This is a very, very limited awareness and has little to offer. If enough effort is used we can isolate any one of our areas of awareness and experience the effects of that point of view.

Under normal conditions we are using our areas of awareness all at once, each one interacting with the other. Most people who think that they are astral projecting are simply shifting their combined awareness to another point within them. As we shift into areas of higher vibratory action we cease to need the lower vibratory areas of awareness. As we shift our attention back toward the physical awareness we engage the areas we set aside before. There are some groups who call this action "Soul traveling," and this term is misleading, too, but closer to the truth. Soul is the observer and is using the other bodies as a vibratory covering while in that plane of action.

Auras

Auras are an interesting study but still a lower teaching. The physical body has a field of energy that radiates from an area of anywhere from an eighth of an inch to several feet from the flesh. The other bodies we carry also have fields of energy surrounding them. As your vibratory rate changes it can be seen in astral awareness as color changes. This energy can be sensed and felt, as well.

Many have attempted to label the colors with meanings as to health, attitude and spiritual unfoldment. As in most metaphysical studies there is a certain amount of truth in this. Rather than trust as fact the observations of others we should develop the ability of seeing auras ourselves and come to our own conclusions as to the meaning of the colors. When we continue on the higher spiritual path we will be less concerned with auras, as we will be able to *know* the information we need. This *knowing* comes from using Soul awareness.

Magick

There are various facets of magic, or magick, the most common being white and black. The only difference is in the intent of the actions. Many metaphysical methods are used by both groups, and both are based primarily in the astral awareness, though mental powers are increasingly playing a part in them.

These are usually organized groups and depend upon the participation and energy of others for their success. Very few magicians, white or black, would survive with their own personal powers. If they were alone who would know that they were magicians? This is not to say that those in magic cannot create an action against you, they can, but only if you allow it. Most magicians have no desire to harm people.

If you sense you are under attack or the influence of anyone, simply envision yourself being surrounded by either a white light or an invisible energy shield, putting most of your energy into the thought. This works against obvious attacks and also with someone who is simply intimidating you with their presence. Many people can have influence over your emotions and thoughts, few of them are magicians, but they can only do this if you allow it.

Many lifetimes ago I studied in a group who centered in white magic, though it was not called that then. There are many occult forces that can be used to gain a desired result, and using these forces is neither good nor bad. The actions carry a karmic burden, as does every Lower World action. The energy fields of the Earth and the planets, with the astral and mental planes, are the source for their power. Combined with the personal energy of those around them these magicians can cause obvious changes. Because it is a limited study and has great potential for misuse I chose to walk away from it. The problem is not in the power itself but how we use it. The power one feels when manipulating forces is strong. Power can be intoxicating and can blind an otherwise well-meaning Soul to the higher goals.

Astrology

This study has been made popular because everyone is seeking some kind of guidance in their lives, and astrology offers explanations as to why we have the behavior patterns we do and what forces will make our life changes happen. Today's astrology is loosely based on an ancient teaching that studied the planet's actions and influence. Missing from both studies is the bigger picture of Soul and the reason for our being here.

There is some truth in astrology as life in the material world, as well as in the rest of the Lower Worlds, works in patterns and cycles. This is part of the mechanism of the creation and while it is interesting, astrology does not begin to touch on the true behind-the-scenes actions in motion. There are forces that hold the Lower Worlds together, some of which science is uncovering, some metaphysics are touching on. Most of the workings are unknown to both groups of study. The daily astrological forecasts in the magazines and papers serve, at best, as comical conversation pieces.

ESP

Extra sensory perception is a catch-all phrase for many abilities, most of them centering on the mental plane. The most common of these is the reading of minds.

This technique is fairly simple, though there are two distinct methods and guidelines involved. The first is taught in metaphysical circles and involves seeing the thought images as they appear around and above the head of the subject. Thought is seen as images by the mind of the person who is reading. The actual form of thought is in vibratory pulse within the band of mental awareness and the mind of the seer translates this into images.

The higher teaching involves working in Soul awareness and we do not have to look about the person's head for their thoughts. We can *know* what we need to know, even if the subject is thousands of miles away. The difference in guidelines is that in the higher teaching we are aware of each person's right to privacy and we do not invade their life in any way without their permission. Not many metaphysical works teach respect for another Soul.

I'm sure you've had many occasions to pick up the phone and hear the voice of someone you were just thinking of. When we know someone can establish a mutual connection then we will know when that person is thinking of us, or perhaps needs us.

If you're not actively involved in these studies it may be somewhat shocking to find that a person can read your thoughts and know your personal questions. Word gets around when someone is able to do this, and before long curious people are flocking to this person for advice. This is the part I don't understand. Does the ability to read someone's mind indicate that the person understands what is read and can give good advice on running our lives, or on spiritual questions? That's a big assumption to make.

Another area of so-called perception is seeing the future. There are several well-known personalities who make their living predicting what will happen to famous people and to the world at large. Their success is limited, at best, because the future is not really predetermined.

The only moment of influence is *now,* and the future is not yet here. We can do much to set up molds that will shape future events in our lives, one way is through creative visualization, but we are not foreseeing the future in this, we are influencing it. It does not take a spiritual scholar to be able to study the patterns in someone's life or in world events and predict a likely outcome. An example would be the grassroots advice that the only thing for sure is death and taxes. I would agree with that advice, as far as Lower World conditions go.

On a higher level, there is an overall structure in the Lower Worlds and a time frame that indicates the likely events that will take place in both man's consciousness and the material worlds. This vision is only known from a very detached viewpoint and involves great insight into not only the lower bodies and spiritual conditions of Soul, but also the mechanical workings of the material worlds. A Master is aware of these conditions and likely events, but He also knows that the future is not yet here and likely events can change. Soul has a choice as to what It will involve Itself in.

One reason for some believing that they can see the future is because of seeing an event in a dream and then having it happen in reality. This could well be the conclusions based on likely patterns and they surface in a dream.

Once I dreamed I was in the thick woods and there I saw a man that I called on in my sales job. He and I were not very close, but we had a friendly relationship. In the dream he appeared drunk or sick, and I could see in his aura a dark, cloudy area in the back of his head. Across the way I saw another image of him; it was his mental body, and he told me that his "brother" was not feeling well and wasn't long for this world. He said he was glad that he didn't have to go through that. A few days later my boss ran into this man on the street and related to me that the man was diagnosed the day before as having a brain tumor. Within a few weeks he died.

I had met the man in another realm of awareness and observed what was happening then. He knew he was sick and it was evident in his aura. I wondered to myself when I awoke if there was any truth to the experience, and if there was, what would happen to him? Did I see the future? No, I saw the present effects at that time and realized a likely outcome. But there are other explanations, too.

When we hold a thought in our awareness strongly it will take form in our lives, often appearing in the dream state and sometimes manifesting in the physical world. It is true that what we fear we can bring into our lives. If we fear something we may carry it actively in our dreams and on into the material plane. The best attitude is one of the middle path, desiring little and fearing nothing.

Bi-location

Bi-location is less talked about because so few people can do this. It is the ability to be in two locations at the same time, or at least appear to be. It is possible to create the image of one's physical self and have it appear in another location. Someone approaching that image would not know it to be a mock-up because it has substance just as the physical body does. Part of the inner awareness controls this body and allows it to communicate with others. This is a relatively complex maneuver and takes a high degree of mastery to accomplish.

More common is the ability to appear to someone in the spiritual body, which could be largely the astral or mental body, and this would look like the person but probably with a shimmering, sparkling mist about it. It requires that the other person be able to sense and be aware of the person in their respective astral or mental awareness. Both of these methods are used by Masters on this plane to work with those who are in their charge.

It is also possible to become invisible to physical senses. This is done by harmonizing vibratory bands within the self with the primary vibratory band of another person or a group of people. When we do this we are not perceived to be another form because we so closely match the vibratory rate of the person, so we become invisible to their senses. This, too, is used by Masters working here, but can be learned by anyone who desires it.

Reading the Signs

Tarot cards, palmistry, face reading, weather omens, reading tea leaves, and handwriting analysis are a few of the forms of reading a person's past and future, or character. The truth of the information lies in the reader's ability to tap into the subject's awareness of their own past and likely future. The cards, or tea leaves, or lines of the palm are mental mock-ups that the reader uses within the mind to tap into that information. We can develop the ability to *know* this information for ourselves and eliminate the middle man.

If I appear to make light of some of these topics you should know that it is not the study that I am critical of; my pointed remarks are aimed at those who use the studies to take advantage of others. Many people love the mystery and intrigue of metaphysics, and this creates those who know nothing of the works but claim to be able to fulfill our natural curiosity, for a price, of course. While this too is an experience for all involved, part of the purpose of this book is to point out a shorter path to walk, and perhaps help in determining the direction to head in.

None of these studies are new to mankind; most have been practiced for tens of thousands of years. They are only a small part of the many abilities we can master while in the Lower Worlds. They are stepping stones to greater realizations even though they are limited in their actions. They cannot in themselves take you into Soul awareness, much less GOD awareness, but you can learn another facet of spiritual truth from them. They are part of the normal progression of

Soul uncovering the mysteries of GOD. There is nothing wrong with metaphysics or participating in it. Each of us decides where we want to place our attention as we determine our goals.

Most discussions of New Age topics center on becoming more aware of our higher self and using these methods to better our lives. We can certainly better our lives through careful use of some of these studies.

It strikes me as funny that several of the more prominent speakers on the New Age are bettering their own lives substantially by charging a lot of money to hear them say less than what's been covered here in just a few words. We owe it to ourselves to question where each study will take us in the end result, and whether that is where we want to go.

Metaphysics aside, this is a New Age in a deeper reality. It has long been known by the Order of Masters that sometime in this century it would probably be necessary to make the information on Soul's true purpose here known to a broader group of people. As Souls have progressed through the ages it has been enough that this secret knowledge was shown to the few who were ready to receive it. The teachings of the Masters over time are evidenced in the greater number of Souls today who are reaching into the higher truths and better able to receive them. Yet, most people do not have the slightest desire to know these truths.

The natural multiplying of vehicles for Soul to inhabit on this planet has served the need of so many who wanted to progress, this plane enabling a faster reconciling of karmic conditions. But with the many vehicles or bodies here, there are Souls who are many lives away from discovering their true self. Man has pushed the level of material knowledge to an almost irresponsible state, having enough information to destroy the planet and not enough insight to prevent it.

Because of this it has been necessary to release this higher study to the open public. It began in the 1920s in Europe and slowly spread to the United States. Many people believe that this higher learning was known openly in China, Tibet and parts of India centuries ago, but it was only realized by the few that the Masters worked with. The study and practice of

Eastern thought has not changed substantially in all the years and is very limited in its awareness.

It was not until the early to mid-1960s did the teachings appear in print before a large audience. It has grown tremendously since then with hundreds of thousands of people having access to the more basic information on Soul. The words are in print and the *One* who is the primary channel for Spirit has made His position known to the world. Behind the scenes there are Masters working with many on the inner planes and also outwardly. But it is always up to each Soul to take this information and combine it with Its experience to realize this knowledge.

The millions of Souls here have the choices before them, and together they will make their future collectively, each Soul deciding Its own future with the whole and individually. The Masters working here will only go so far in maintaining the order of this world, the rest is left up to those who struggle here.

All of this is the play of life, and no matter the result Soul will survive and continue on the spiritual path. Some courses may appear better than others for the short term, but in the big picture they don't matter as much as some want to believe. One should be more concerned with knowing one's self as Soul before trying to save the world. As many do this, the level of spiritual unfoldment can be such that the combined responsibility for our actions can save this world.

This is the New Age of greater understanding, a time as never before on this planet. More information is available more freely than ever before, more than on any other lower plane of awareness. The expanded interest in metaphysics can be the catalyst for many to take the next step within, and in this each study has its place in the journey of Soul.

21

Man,
Woman, and Love

You may relate to the image of yourself as being either male or female, but Soul is neither. It is the gender form taken that carries with it the emotional and mental influences that can cause you to perceive yourself as being male or female. What you believe to be true about yourself will continue to be true until you replace the concept with one that is of equal conviction, if not stronger.

Each of us has lived in bodies on this planet and other realms as both the male and female aspect. Generally Soul will take a gender form for several lives and then change to the other for several lives, and then repeat this process until the balance of spiritual experience is found. Soul is challenged by the experiences of being subjected to a primarily positive influence and then a negative influence, in the forms of male and female. Each life holds many opportunities for Soul to establish new insight.

Think of the complex realm of factors that challenges Soul in each life. There are karmic ties to other Souls that It will interact with; there are karmic responsibilities to settle within Itself, plus the overall situation Soul will be born into. Assuming a male or female emotional and physical shell often blinds Soul into believing it is that body form and nothing else, giving It the challenge to discover that It is really Soul.

Soul is neither male nor female, it is made of matter that is beyond the material worlds. Part of the process Soul uses to gain experience while in the lower worlds is one of positive and negative, male and female.

We live our life as primarily grounded in one field, either positive/male, or negative/female. The male and female essence is in the emotional and physical bodies. Being that, in these material worlds, there are both elements found in every form, and we are comprised of both, too.

If you are in the male body now you may think of this as being seven parts masculine and three parts feminine, for each of us has elements of both within us. The female form can be thought of as seven parts feminine and three parts masculine. This is an over-simplification of a multifaceted and complex subject, but it serves our purpose here.

As Soul matures It breaks free of being overly influenced by the bodies It is grounded in and lives as the true self that It is. Soul is neither gender, and yet It can be influenced by both positive and negative while in a body. The goal can be thought of as attaining five parts male and five parts female, or a balancing of the positive and negative aspects.

It is this instinctive struggle to find balance that often brings man and woman together. Man seeks to balance his seven parts male with the woman's three parts male, and yet because of Soul's distant memory, he also tries to join his three parts female with the woman's seven parts. The woman does much the same. Emotional and mental conditioning support the combination of man and woman, and all of us feel compelled to be with our opposite. If this seems confusing, realize that it is no more confusing than any other aspect of men and women. Relationships are really not based on logic; they are based on deep internal emotional and spiritual needs, needs for experience that very few ever consciously realize. Soul craves knowledge, and It seeks the experiences that will bring It closer to the Source. The emotional element found in all of us is sometimes called the animal instinct because it is a primal and narrow band of awareness that carries a powerful influence in our lives.

In this instinctive struggle to balance the positive and

negative aspects It has aquired, It pairs with the opposite. Eventually Soul will discover that It can contain the balance in Itself and does not need another to make It whole. But what a marvelous way for Soul to gain experience! Think of how much you have gained from being that closely involved with another Soul. You could have gained the same spiritual experiences on your own but sharing the conditions of physical and emotional conditions speeds up the process of spiritual realization.

Of course, this should dispell the notion of Soul mates. We do not have one Soul we must join with or forever roam unhappy. We can balance the positive and negative forces all by ourselves. Though we have loved and gained from many who were close to us, it is a personal balance that we must accomplish alone.

Not only is the physical body grounded in its vibratory rate by male or female form, the emotional body carries a gender pattern as well. So does the mind, though less so. To answer those who maintain that male and female behavior is a product of upbringing and conditioning, that is true to some extent. But that is a surface view of the situation.

Soul is neither male or female, but takes the body form of one or the other, matched with the emotional body of the same gender base, and the distant past experiences of having been in that form before. You can raise a small child to be the opposite of its body form but it will most probably still carry the traits found in what its emotional base is. Let us not be blinded by our conceptions of what male and female is. Male is a positive base, and female is a negative base. They each carry aspects of the same force but expressed in different ways and extremes. One is no better than the other, no greater, no closer to GOD. Both aspects enable Soul to experience what It needs to be complete. When these emotional elements are confused and past elements are sensed without the overall understanding of the process of Soul's realization, Soul may be attracted to a body form that matches Its own. With time the experience will balance the emotional level of Soul, much as takes place within the traditional pairing of Souls.

Soul will eventually overcome the influence of Its body forms and be both, and yet be beyond both by being neither form. It will balance the positive and negative aspects in all areas of Its experience in this world.

Many people wonder if a woman can attain Mastership and the answer is no, but neither can a man. It is Soul who balances all the forces and frees Itself from the attachments and becomes the Master. At that point It may carry the body form It had as long as It chooses to work in the Lower Worlds. In the Higher Worlds there is no body form. There are Masters who carry the body form of a woman.

While Souls do live life together for reasons other than emotional, this primal awareness is what bonds most relationships. The love we practice in the lower worlds is largely a conditional agreement combined with the fulfillment of an emotional need. "I will love you if you will do this for me," or "If you loved me you wouldn't act that way." When we feel that we are being loved we feel less alone and more complete. Often this conditional agreement is not expressed openly but is understood and reinforced by the values of society. Please understand that I'm not condemning this. I know that what appears to be the strongest love in the world can be subtly conditional. This is all in place, and this is another way we experience what we must.

Man and woman do not have to express a conditional love; they can give total and complete respect and space to each other. They can love the other no matter what happens and allow the other to grow at their own pace. It takes a mature and confident person to give this love, someone who understands that they themselves need that same kind of love in return, and it must be given to be received. This is a higher form of love, a reflection of the totally unconditional love that is found in the Higher Worlds. Here we will express our sense of that higher love through our emotional selves, and this is a real challenge. Higher love involves giving, not taking. Unconditional love requires being responsible for our own actions and allowing the other to go through what they must to grow, loving them all the same with a nonconditional love.

Each one of us carries a personal understanding of what we know love to be; that is the love we have experienced in our lives and the love we may wish to have.

All Masters have spoken of love and their words are taken with the understanding we each hold. There is the emotional force and pulse of love, there is the mental recognition of what love is and can be, and there are the hundreds of splintered emotional and mental variations of love known in this world. While the Masters know their words will be understood within these frameworks, the source and understanding of their love is much different. The love they base their words on is the highest love of all, the Love of GOD.

It can only be experienced to be understood, but to attempt to explain I will say that when one stands in the presence of GOD ITSELF there are two overwhelming realizations in proportions never before known. They are Power and Love. Every particle of one's being vibrates with the overwhelming Power that emits from the core of the GOD World, while at the same time knowing that the power is based with unquestioned acceptance of your presence: Love.

You know that you belong with IT, that you are part of IT, that IT is you, and you will always from that moment on be less than a second away from IT. You feel humble indeed, knowing that you are such a small part of the Work, but you are an important part in the meaning of Soul's journey. This is the Love of GOD, the realization that you are part of it all, that IT is part of you, and that every Soul is part of IT, too.

Another realization takes place as we learn of the Higher Worlds and that is freedom. When we can break the illusions and travel in awareness within the worlds of GOD, we are truly free. This realization of freedom will be expressed through every aspect of our lives and affects how we interrelate with other Souls.

With this understanding our entire concept of the worlds can change, the way we view ourselves, our friends, and all the strangers we will encounter.

The Love of GOD is unconditional in that one has only to accept IT to know IT, one has only to realize what already exists. We can, in turn, feel this same unemotional acceptance for all life, especially Soul. It is not necessary to feel emotionally in love with the world, in fact it is better to emotionally love as few people as possible because of the risks of attachments. It is better to channel this unconditional love, or good will, toward everyone, and take the few special Souls into our hearts.

This Love of GOD is the meaning of all we are and can be; it is the fabric that wraps the worlds with a warmth of understanding and acceptance that cannot be matched.

Behind the outer and inner relationship that a man and woman seem to share is the reality that two Souls are interchanging experience and working with the needs of their own spiritual search. They may assist each other with the experiences and the lessons learned, and they may find that they have grown apart. I do not believe that man and woman cannot stay together throughout a life for they certainly can if they desire it. The guilt and sense of failure that goes with two people deciding not to stay together is a product of our society and emotional nature. Everything changes all the time. Two people can change together and help each other grow or they may find that they have grown apart and would be better served to go alone. Two Souls can experience life in order to gain spiritual freedom, not just to simply be a man and a woman struggling with the family, mortgage, jobs and growing old.

We are wise to see our children through the view of the big picture, as Souls entering this world for experience. The small picture is the day-to-day challenges of growing up, cutting teeth, learning to walk, first days of school, boy and girl friends, borrowing the car, college tuition, and paying for the wedding. Yes, we must deal with all of this as it happens, moment to moment. But we are wise to regain our perspective by remembering the purpose of it all, the Big Picture. Soul.

22

Paul

The man who wrote the books and discourses I've referred to is Paul Twitchell, and He is from the long line of Masters that has carried the Truth of these Higher Teachings across the checkered past of the material world. Paul was charged with making the teachings public, while before they were passed from the Teacher to a chosen few followers.

He wrote articles and books and began lecturing to small groups. Soon He wrote discourses and taught the basic principles to all who wanted to grow with that study. Another important aspect of His work was to develop a system of spiritual exercises that would accelerate the process of shifting awareness. His work was not an easy task, and sometimes He did not feel Himself worthy to carry the tremendous responsibility. You see, each one who studied His words was under His protection and guidance, and He watched their progress and assisted in ways that few would believe. Though He had attained GOD awareness He was always living in a humble attitude, knowing that He was but a servant of GOD. Slowly He developed the ability to balance this heavy responsibility with the physical demands on His life, and a new outer teaching evolved.

Paul is the founder of the outer teaching that still exists today, but when I first read His book in my car that afternoon He had already left His physical body five years before.

It was He that worked with me off and on when I was a child. I later recognized it was Him by the rhythm of His words in His writings, and He continued to assist me after I actively pursued His teachings.

When I first entered the outer teachings He had founded, I had read every book He had written before I met anyone else in the group, except for Hutch. There was a small meeting room where some of the members of the group would meet, and I should define the picture here. The people in this study were just like you and I; they worked normal jobs and many were professional people. They didn't wear robes and shave their heads unless they were from a culture that dressed that way. You probably have met half a dozen of them and don't even know it. No more than you could tell a Baptist from a Catholic at a glance, could you tell one of them from anyone else.

The meeting room was simple enough, a desk and bookcase filled with books, a few chairs and a sofa in the corner. Nothing fancy, and there was certainly no vast amount of money changing hands. The group has no priesthood, no temples, and no television ministry to support. The whole idea is to put the information in front of anyone who desires it, and the individual takes the information and grows with it. They have classes and cassette tapes, and while there is an outer organization it is always up to the individual to grow at his own pace. Many people study the works privately, rarely meeting with a group. The outer organization provides the information while the Master works with Soul on the inner planes to couple the information with spiritual experience.

I was in the meeting room one Thursday morning when an older woman, perhaps in her late sixties, came up the walk. She wore a full, brown skirt and bright flowery blouse, and an emerald green beret. I was surprised when she walked in the door. I was introduced and when I took her hand an electrical charge went up my arm and settled at the base of my neck. I tried to not look shocked but I was, you know. I asked her to sit and join us, though it was I who needed to sit down. I will never forget the light in her eyes. I found out that she was one of the original group that Paul worked with when He first started. She carried a *knowing* with her that surpassed the awareness of most people. She was somewhat aloof and not very active in the outer group anymore, but she had continued in her spiritual progress.

Two years later my personal world fell to pieces, and I was looking for a room to rent. Someone gave me an address in an older part of Atlanta and I could only smile with a deep reassurance when she opened the door. I rented her small room for a few months, and many evenings we would sit and talk. One night she opened an old trunk and brought out personal letters and manuscripts, and before I read what they were I could sense a familiar feeling and oddly, a familiar scent in the air. The letters were from Paul to her, and she had a few of His early manuscript copies that would later become His books. She missed Him terribly, and her life was not as full since He had walked away from this world.

Paul was an incredible person; His physical energy alone would amaze most. And He was a character, living His physical life with a fullness and reality of *being* here. The image many people held of Him was quite different than who He really was. He usually dressed in casual slacks and a short-sleeved shirt, a pale blue. He was a simple appearing man, though He held the secrets of the ages within Him.

He had a slight southern accent, being raised in the South, but He had traveled the world many times in His research to work into the Mastership. What I know of Paul is not just from what others have said, it is from knowing Him in the present moment. Describing Him as He was in a physical body, and as He is on the inner planes leads to problems in whether to use present or past tense when referring to Him.

Paul is a Master of the Highest Order, and He carries a love that is felt as comfort and seen as power in times of need. This love is from the GOD Worlds, and He guides thousands into a greater understanding of their lives.

Paul's presence was in her house almost constantly. My personal world, my emotions, were shaken going through a divorce and financial upheaval, and it was no accident that I found a room in her house. Paul appeared to her often. I talked with Him three years earlier in the simple hut in the forest, but often He had been a distant Teacher in my inner life. My first inner Master in this life was Ramini, and it was He who appeared in my living room years earlier and laid the groundwork for what Paul would give me later.

I had thought of Paul and my other Teachers as being outside of myself, and in doing that I was isolated and shut off from many experiences I might have gained. I thought other people were having better inner realizations and en-counters with the Masters. I remember thinking that one day I would be able to realize a certain understanding or visit a certain plane in my spiritual awareness. Everything was out-side of myself, not readily available in the *here* and *now.*

That is one of the subtlest illusions we face. As long as we believe that something is beyond us then it will be, whether it is a material goal in this world or a spiritual experience. Everything we know is within us, and all we can be is within us, and every plane in the vast worlds of GOD is within us, *here* and *now.* We have only to be *here,* right *now,* and *act* in the power that we already hold. These are mere words printed here, but the realization of what I just said can change your life forever.

As in all endeavors, a little experience goes a long way in giving us confidence. With confidence we can begin to relax in our task, and in relaxing we can accomplish more with less wear and tear on our energy. This is true of spiritual studies, and all of us will discover it with time. I say the time can be right now, are you ready?

The Master has a way of appearing all of a sudden and in-viting you to travel to a new experience with Him. The time is *now,* not some point in the future. The future is not yet here, we have only *now.*

I left her small room a few months after finding it and went through many changes in the next three years. I seemed to be on the edge of realizing the truth of what I was going through, but always on the edge. I had lost my home, a mar-riage, the close contact with my daughters, but I was still responsible for their needs. There were periods where I didn't have enough money to rent a room, so I slept in the back seat of my old car. And even though I worked two jobs at once, in order to eat, I still had to sell my blood for plasma, my obligations were so great. There were moments when I seriously considered fleeing to South America, but I didn't have enough money to make it there. Of course, I couldn't have left my daughters with no support.

Eventually I realized that I had to learn about attachments, that I was holding on to material images for my inner security. Those had to be ripped from me before I could really rely on just me, my own ability as Soul. I had to even out my emotions, balance them though I felt pulled from every angle. I had to let go of what I was holding on to which was the dependence on everything outside of myself. I had only me left, and even though others may have wanted to save me, to love and take care of me at times, they could not make up for what I lacked inside. I could not believe that I was enough, that I had the power to change my world by myself. It was the hardest task I had ever faced.

You may not think of yourself as being attached to material goods, and perhaps you are not. After all, it is not hard to understand that it isn't the object that's good or bad, it's the value and the attachment we place in it. Most of us admit that we could live without most of our possessions if we had to. We also know that objects do not make us wealthy or truly happy. But do we know about the emotional and mental structures that we feel secure in, the worlds we have built around us that are safe and familiar?

The most subtle attachments come in the form of our concepts of the world we live in and depend upon. Our home, our friends, our work, our families. We often see these things as extensions of ourselves, and when they change we feel our secure world threatened.

As we grow stronger in the awareness of who we really are, we begin to be more challenged by the negative forces. It is not unusual for the truth seeker to find turmoil and constant change in his world. We are left to find comfort where we can, and eventually we see that there is no place and no one who can give us comfort. We are alone. The only comfort to be found is from within ourselves.

I have found that the hardest changes come very subtly and strike us when we are least prepared. We are not aware of how involved we are with the forms we have created in our lives until we are challenged with change. The mind and emotions work very differently but they share the trait of forming patterns that they remain with or ruts of behavior. So many of our decisions and feelings are based on past responses to like situations, and these reactions are seldom based on knowingness. They are most commonly based on fear or insecurity. One problem I faced during this period was the surfacing of my previous life's worst traits. These problems had not been resolved and when under stress I would lapse into the thinking of that life, the behavior, and sometimes I would speak in the accent I had then. The attachments of that life bridged into this one, and I had to overcome this.

When we desire to change a certain condition we find little trouble in adapting to the new environment these changes provide. But when we feel forced to change we usually resist, feeling threatened and manipulated. What we fail to see is that most occurrences in our lives are the direct result of some action on our part. In this we need to see the area of our responsibility for our actions and their consequences. Other changes in life are the result of actions on the part of others, and in this we have to realize that we can only control ourselves. We must learn to adapt to the ever-present shifting of events in this world.

Many feelings are involved in adapting to change. Sometimes change is welcome, but it is more apt to bring the cries of "not fair," "what did I do to deserve this," or "they made me go through this."

Though I doubt it makes anyone feel better, I will point out that in conflict we have a chance to grow, in that we may gain much insight in new experiences. The causes of change may include karmic actions, which we are responsible for, or the attraction of the negative force.

I do not like to emphasize the negative aspect, but we should know that it serves the function of teaching us. The negative force is charged with the action of meeting our positive action. These forces colliding causes conflict, to be sure. We may grow by meeting and overcoming the challenge, which may involve much upset and confusion before gaining our control.

There is no shelter from change; we cannot really avoid the conflict of ourselves and the negative force. If we choose to be passive and give in to all obstacles then we will eventually be dissatisfied and unhappy. In our effort to change that condition we will bring on the change process again. Many people believe that they can settle for less than they want or deserve in their lives, but in time everyone will reach out for what is theirs. We are reaching for control of our lives and for the peace that comes with accomplishment and knowledge.

I cannot tell you that I met every challenge with confidence. There were many times when I did not know where I would end up, or why. I saw myself pulled in many directions, and I think the hardest part sometimes is watching those you love hurt in the crossfire of these times. But I had to go on, and I had to find a way of slowly working through every situation. Some were more graceful than others, and I can say that I have been the prize fool on more occasions than one.

It was in this time period that I experienced violating the Law of Silence. Ramini had told me of this law many years before, but I was not thinking of His teaching at that time.

I made the mistake one evening of boasting about some of my past exploits on the inner planes, and I got strange looks from everyone seated at the table with me. They had no idea what I was talking about and must have thought I was crazy. There was no need for that outburst, as I was only talking to hear myself talk.

The reaction of Spirit was swift and exact to my action of violating the spiritual law. I suffered nightmares that night as I developed one of my famous "fevers of unknown origin," as the doctors call them. I suffered with a high fever for almost a week, largely because my vibratory rate had dropped to a point where I was out of balance in my Lower World bodies. What vibratory rate I maintained in this time period was lowered by me revealing aspects of the inner teaching.

The Law of Silence involves keeping secret the inner teachings of the Master, and every direct act and word of the Master is a teaching. The reason for this is that the teaching is for you, alone, and not for the world. Often there is a charged word given, or higher realization expressed in a phrase, or an image. To reveal this to someone else, no matter their spiritual place, is a violation of the Law. You can lose the energy and effect of the teaching by revealing it to someone else.

Revealing the secret words can also lead to envy and misunderstanding on the part of those you talk to, involving you with their problems, and even their karma. The person you tell may not be in a position to hold the information at that time, and it could lead to problems in emotional and mental balance.

Talking about a public, or written work of a Master is acceptable because the information is processed by the Master to be absorbed on a broad scale. The one on one encounters with the Master, whether on the inner or outer reality, are private teachings for you only.

Special vibratory arrangements and adjustments were made so that I would be able to share the essence of the experiences presented in this book. Part of this work involves taking complete responsibility for the information given, even when presented on such a broad scale. Many years ago the Masters directed that I write down select teachings so that I would be able to share them one day, even though I did not fully understand the plans at the time.

A full three years went by with me rarely seeing anyone in the organized group. During that period I would sometimes cry out for direction; I would pray for the Master to appear to me in a dream to tell me what to do. The loneliness of knowing that not another person understood was overwhelming. There was total silence from the Master during this time. But He was there, He was helping me by allowing me to gain this experience for myself, because I still asked that I be shown what was needed in my life. The Master allowed me to have what I needed.

I slowly assembled a new set of values based on the new

inner strength I was developing. With time I balanced the emotions that I had been reacting to and began to feel what I, as Soul, wanted to feel. There were many lonely moments in making the new decisions I had to make. Wiser for the experiences, I chose to go on, deeper into the teachings. I was free of most of the attachments and aware of those that remained.

You may not have to experience this, it is not required, but it is one form of life experience that gives us the spiritual realizations we may need. Yours may take a much different form, and you may come to understand your attachments slowly in your life.

To live in this world we must be attached, in a sense. We love other people, and in this there is some attachment. Paul said, "Love who you must and give your good will to all." He was speaking of the attachments that emotional love can carry. To have the few primary holdings here is acceptable, as long as we understand their place and can release them when the time comes. This is very subtle.

To be free of any pull in this world, to be able to walk away if needed, is one of the most comforting aspects of living here. We can become a law unto ourselves, because we determine completely what will be in our lives.

One day I turned around and felt different, a little cocky at having survived that long. I had just rented a small studio, had just enough money to do that, even if I had no furniture. I looked about the room and felt better for it all and started laughing. I didn't want any furniture; I really didn't want any more than I had right then; I was content in my few material belongings. I was content in having me, all within myself. For the first time in my existence I felt whole.

My clothes were a bit dated, the kitchen had a pot and a plate and a fork. I had two boxes of books and papers, and I was happy and laughing. I did not have a relationship with a woman in my life, and usually I worked too many hours to have a social life.

As the months went on I remained happy and found a nice wooden box on the curb that became a table, and someone donated a nice old desk to write on. How could life be any better than that? I used to stand at the porch door and stare into the night and smile.

One night I heard someone laughing across the room. It was Paul. He liked the decor, but thought it might be good to have a couple of chairs so we could sit and talk sometime. In a matter of days two chairs appeared and from a most unlikely source, but there they were. He used to remark that it reminded Him of so many of His rooms, and the simpler the better. I never asked Him where He had been, why He had not helped me through those terrible times. He had helped me.

Over the next year Paul would meet me in the spiritual worlds almost nightly. Many of the lessons that I thought I knew mentally were experienced fully on the inner planes.

I should point out here the difference between the presence of the physical and inner Master. The Master that maintains a physical body on this planet is capable of projecting His inner body to another inner location where He may be realized by someone who has the ability to *see* with inner sight. He may also appear in the appropriate form in any of the worlds of GOD. He may at times project in the physical world a mock-up, or imaged body that appears and feels physical, though His actual body is at another physical location. Ramini supports a physical body and does appear physically to others at times, though most of His work is on the inner planes of awareness.

A Master who has left the physical body works on the inner planes and bases His work wherever He chooses within the other worlds of GOD. While this Master is aware of the physical conditions of the planet and the Souls here that He works with, you must shift your awareness to where He is to be in His presence. It is rare that this Master will appear in the physical world of awareness, as this would require lowering the vibratory rate to a point that could create a negative condition on His work.

In writing this book I have tried to relate the experiences as I perceived them, yet my words are based on my thoughts, which are material in nature. The reality of the experience is that the event happened within some point of my awareness, though not necessarily in the physical world. Paul was very much aware of the physical changes my life went through, but when I speak of Him appearing to me it was I who shifted awareness to where He was. I sensed His connection with me at that moment, much like a voice calling my name and instantly became aware of Him.

Many of the physical experiences I've described seem to take place in the main room of my studio. I would sense His call and then we would often sit in the chairs and talk, though this was happening on another plane of awareness. At first I didn't realize what was taking place because the environment did not seem to change. Because the planes are reflective of the next higher realm, it was simple for Him to allow that the discourses take place in a setting that I felt comfortable in. I always felt lighter and highly charged in Paul's presence so I didn't notice the slight difference in the appearance of the room. At one point He explained what was happening, but only after I asked how He was able to visit me.

When the experience would begin my physical body paralleled the movements of the inner body. When the visit was concluded I would return to the physical awareness of the body either sitting in the chair or on the edge of the bed or wherever I had been when the inner experience ended. Once you become accustomed to shifting awareness you change environments without noticing the change. There is no break in the awareness of Soul, just in the Lower World senses. When I refer to Paul appearing to me I am speaking from the immediate viewpont within the state of awareness at that moment.

He suggested that I might want to explain this in my writings one day. I was a bit taken aback by that statement because at that time I had no idea of how I could possibly write down these experiences. He helped me with this work, as He did with so many other areas of my growth. I have been blessed.

23

The
Warrior

I was returning from a trip to Boston, where I had visited a close friend, and my thoughts were not focused as I stared at the carpet of billowing clouds under the jet traveling at thirty thousand feet over the earth. My attention was suddenly drawn to the sound of water moving by my feet when I found myself in the presence of Paul. We were sitting under an old, snarled tree on the bank of a dark river, somewhere in what appeared to be Northern India.

I looked at Him as He spoke.

"One must see himself as the warrior as he travels the spiritual road. There are many who would destroy the truth seeker."

I felt puzzled by His statement, and must have shown it in my expression.

"You have faced danger from time to time, do you remember?"

I did recall several incidents from another time, when life was dangerous to those who practiced the forbidden beliefs. And there were times in other lives when magic was used against me. Even though there were a few episodes of danger in this life, I hadn't thought of myself as being a warrior. Paul did not wait long for me to answer.

"The Soul who is close to finding GOD will have many, who are negative based, try to detain It. Recall when you traveled alone across these lands. You were open to the experience, but your goal was to survive in an unknown world. The tiger stalked you, the python watched as you thought you were moving silently through the bush. Once you walked into the dug-out trap for the tiger, and you barely climbed to safety. The tiger watched and would have attacked."

As I stared into His eyes a slight smile crossed His expression. I knew that He, or another Master, had held the tiger back that time, though I also knew that He would not admit it to me.

"But in recent moments, have you not been attacked in your dreams?"

I slowly answered. "Yes, not long ago two men approached me asking for directions, and then they tried to force me into a car."

"What did you do?" He asked.

"I ran into a shopping mall close by and eluded them. At one point they were close to catching me and I shifted my attention to a different point."

"You disappeared?"

"I suppose it appeared to them that I had disappeared."

"Do you know who they were?"

I thought about that for a moment, and concluded that I didn't know the men. I had not taken the experience seriously, thinking that it was simply a dream.

Paul knew what I was thinking. "Don't take your dreams so lightly, and there is no such thing as coincidence or accident. The men were agents of the negative force, though they did not know why you were to be captured; they just knew their instructions. You acted swiftly and saved yourself, leaving that region of the astral world. Do you recall the time you were rammed by another car when you were driving? That, too, was in the astral world. It was no accident, and your back was strained so badly that you felt it in your physical body.

"What I'm pointing out to you is that as long as you are in the Lower Worlds you should be aware that there are those, who represent the negative force, who would keep you from your duties as a representative of this work. They are not to be feared, because they really cannot hurt you if you are aware of their presence and meet them with your energy. As you channel more of the positive force and raise your vibratory rate as you gain awareness, you will attract the negative force in greater levels because it will attempt to off-set the positive. By understanding this you should overcome any fear associated with the process.

"On the other hand, don't take the negative force lightly, either. You have been trained in defense when attacked, you know how to act instead of hesitating. The negative side can upset your physical and emotional bodies to a point where you may have to leave them behind. That would change the work you have on the planet.

"Perhaps more of a threat would be the subtle aspects of the negative side. You make your way actively in the world, and you are very involved in physical contacts with people. That, in itself, can drain your energy, but many conditions that present themselves as problems are the work of the negative force in an effort to keep your attention on the problems and off of your true work.

"You can use mockups to protect yourself, but the Master rarely needs these. He stands in power with the awareness that He holds, and the attack is repelled by His energy.

"From time to time you may choose to allow an attack on your Lower World body, perhaps in an illustration for one who needs the experience or in order to offset the karma of one you choose to help. Make a knowing decision as to what you will allow, knowing that the negative is devoted to hindering the work of the Master. This is the play of life.

"So, in this light, I say that each spiritual seeker must be prepared, as is the warrior, and provide the balance in the forces of these worlds. The attitude should be one of detach-ment and yet determination, of alertness and of giving; of good will and of power in the positive forces. It is this balance that allows you to equal your karmic responsibilities, to free your attachments, and gains you the GOD Worlds."

As I nodded my head in understanding my forehead touched the inner window of the airplane and brought my attention to the winding roads of the landscape below. When I landed in Atlanta a few minutes later I was at first very watchful and apprehensive of the strangers around me. After a while I laughed at my oversensitivity and relaxed my attitude to be one of confidence and openness to life. I was in control of my world, aware of the play of forces all around me.

When I walked what seemed like ten miles to my car I got in to find that it wouldn't start. I rested my head on the steering wheel in amazement of the situation before me. I tried the ignition again and the engine turned over and started. As I hurried out of the whirling energy of the airport I discovered that my headlights would not work, and I drove twenty-five miles to the studio in total darkness.

Since that time I have been aware of many incidents that were reactions of the negative force to the positive flow that I carry. The physical task of writing this book has taken just over two years of composing the thoughts into words, and once I started many obstacles got in the way.

I have always been rather healthy, but after two months of actively outlining the initial chapters my body was sidelined as I returned home from a few days of rest in Mexico. I had an unknown condition with high fever that kept me hospitalized for almost a week and in bed for another ten days. Six months later, after making good progress on the book, my body developed appendicitis, and I was back in the hospital for surgery.

I've had entire chapters of this book wiped from the word processing computer disc with no logical explanation. I'll not be stopped for long by such tactics, and while other conditions were worked out in the physical process of ill health, I know that these were largely attempts to stop the book.

When we realize the role of the negative force, that it is charged with the task of conflict with the positive, we cease to fear it. This situation is a condition of being in the Lower Worlds and the wise truth-seeker knows that there is neither good nor bad in positive and negative forces. There is but difference.

The Master is subject to all these forces while in the

Lower Worlds and must balance His world accordingly. Many attempts have been made on the lives of several of the Masters I have known, and some of them were partially successful in that the Master allowed the incident to happen for a purpose. Paul is said to have been poisoned while in Spain and suffered for months afterward. Some have said that it broke His body down and contributed to His physical death a short time later. He indicated to a few people that He had known of the attempt in advance but had not stopped it because it was necessary to circumstances that He was working with. The details to this incident will likely never be made public, largely because so few could accept the true explanation. The inner workings of the Masters are sometimes hard to understand in the limited framework of our minds and emotions. Most people would be shocked and amazed at how much of Himself the Master gives to those He is charged to assist.

Sometimes those who are actively seeking on the path will attempt to do the greatest harm to the Master. While the two forces are aspects of Spirit, which is of GOD ITSELF, the Master knows that many Souls are blinded by overindulgence in either energy. Lack of knowledge of the power of these forces leads to confusion and conflict for not just the person involved, but for those around the person, as the person strikes out.

Out of responsibility and love the Master will assist those who are not balanced and who ask for His help. The Master knows that when Soul is saturated in the positive flow, over too long a period, It will become disoriented and risks losing the awareness It holds. This can be a critical time for the spiritual seeker, and all too often the negative force fills the role of balancing the person back to middle ground. Once this takes place Soul may not realize the negative influence for what it is, mistaking the energy that balanced It as being positive. Over time the negative energy lowers the vibratory rate of Soul and subtly guides Its actions. If requested in time, the Master can balance Soul by other methods and gradually lead It back to knowing Itself. Becoming overbalanced can happen to one new on the path, and the Master knows that it can happen to Him, as well, if He allows it.

A similar event took place several years ago with a Master who became overbalanced with the force and fell in awareness. This is not commonplace, but it does happen. After repeated attempts to work with this Master it was deemed necessary to force him from the Order because of the disruptive nature of his actions. Today he leads a group of followers who are very devoted to him, and he does hold power, though many believe it is based largely in the negative. The challenge is in deciding the truth behind all these events as he is a public figure and was a leader of thousands when it happened, and many people today look to him for guidance.

The Master is subject to all conditions that every other Soul faces, and there is no resting point of having gained all the awareness of GOD. GOD is not a limited power or understanding and is ever expanding. While in the Lower Worlds, every Soul, no matter the awareness, must be as the warrior.

24

Gulf Shores

The job I worked was demanding because I needed to succeed in making a small company grow. I was given an opportunity to develop a market for a group of products and if successful I would share in the profits. My personal expenses had been very high in relation to my income, so with this chance to increase my earnings I devoted a great deal of time and energy over a few years to the business. The efforts were successful and my income increased enough to allow me to move into the studio, though allowed for little else.

Sometimes I would have to drive to the surrounding states and call on accounts personally. The long drives were good times to be alone and reflect on all the changes in my life, or more importantly, what I had gained from the changes.

Just before the last series of business trips I had a feeling deep within that I might not return. It seemed that something was about to happen. The feelings were so strong that I was moved to handwrite a will to whoever would find it. This ended up being a letter to my daughters, because I had no belongings to leave to anyone. I didn't really know what to think about what I was feeling, but I wasn't upset.

After returning from the trips unharmed I wondered just what was happening inside. After taking a long walk one night it became apparent to me that the feeling that I was about to die was my conscious mind realizing that a part of my outer structure and image of my life was ending. I was giving up some very subtle attachments regarding my attitude about myself. The ways I saw myself being were no more and the mind was threatened by those changes and perceived a coming loss. Realizing that, I tore up the letters and have never sensed again that I would die. I know now that I have a choice in living here and I will leave this world when all my work is accomplished, not before.

Periodically I would take a few days off and drive to the Gulf of Mexico. I stayed in a state campground that was on the ocean for a few dollars a night and spent most of the time walking on the beach. The ocean can express many forms and vibratory rates, but the level usually felt is relatively high. The Sound can be heard in the waves breaking on the beach, and the rhythm of the tides is somewhat like the current of Spirit coming into the Lower Worlds and then going back into the GOD Worlds. Remember that everything is a dim reflection of the next higher plane, and all Lower World images have a basis of existence in the GOD Worlds.

Many Masters live close to the ocean because of the higher vibratory rate, just as many live in the remote mountains across the planet for the same reason. The Master can overcome negative environments but it is a load to carry that need not always be there.

One morning I awoke suddenly in my tent and could hear only an owl hooting from near the bay side of the campground. I dressed and walked the sand path that cut through the sea grass near the beach. I had not brought my watch but I knew the sun was only an hour off the horizon. The tide had washed seaweed and broken planks high on the beach, but at that moment the ocean seemed unusually still. There was little sound and almost no breeze.

I turned to my left and Azjur Ramini was walking with me.

"Do you remember when we were in the little valley? We would leave after meditation each morning and climb down the steep path to Shantok. We would knock on the doors of the huts and the women would give us food."

I smiled as I remembered those moments. "I would sometimes be embarrassed that we would beg."

"We were not begging, we were giving the village the blessings of the holy men, we were next to GOD."

"Was that true? Were we next to GOD?"

He laughed quietly to Himself. "They believed that we were, and they took great comfort in supporting the holy men because we meditated and fasted for them and their lives. GOD looked favorably on their crops and animals. It was a fair exchange."

"I was not so holy then. I don't think I'm so holy now, either," I remarked. I shuddered for an instant in recalling that I had walked away from His teaching because I could not find GOD with Him then.

"I don't think of myself as being holy. I know what other people call holy, but I've rarely been that. Perhaps some would call us holy by the way we appear or act. How do you see yourself?"

At that moment I felt very alone. I wasn't lonely, rather I knew that there was no one who understood what I had been through, except perhaps, Ramini and Paul. I stopped walking and faced the breaking waves. I could not speak.

"It has been your experience. I've watched you grow through some of those times. My path is a little different, I had a slower pace in time and lifestyle, though the discipline was greater. Once I spent an entire winter alone in the upper regions of the mountains with no shelter or food. My Master sent me out to find my survival factor. I lived under an overhanging rock and warmed myself in my robes and in my attitude. I fasted as much as possible and ate bark and twigs periodically. Thank GOD it was a mild winter!"

I laughed. My path had been very different, though some of my early training did call for periods of darkness and silence, and I did spend months alone in the wild at one point but in the warmth of the summer.

As He continued we started to walk. "But an interesting change came from that experience. When I came back to find my Master in the Spring I had nothing to say, and I did not want to talk to anyone. When I first went into the mountains

I was terribly lonely, though all of us in the group knew we had to undergo that test and believed that we would be strong. I did not think I would survive after a couple of weeks, but then I had no choice because the snows blocked all the paths down the mountain. I would have died trying to live, so I lived when I thought I would die."

There was a sparkle in His eyes as He spoke.

"To live I had to redefine my world of life and look to what was available for me to use. I had myself and little else, but it was sufficient to survive! After realizing the inner power of life that I held I had little to say to anyone else. My words were coarse and the world of men, even though they were my brothers in the group, was superficial. I felt very alone in what I knew, yet I saw the aloneness in my Master's eyes. A distant, faraway gaze that no one else, except those who shared the experience, could understand. It was not the experience of being alone itself, it was the truth of the inner life that was revealed and separated me from everyone else."

He did understand my aloneness. I had not discovered it two centuries ago in the wild, but rather in the city of lives over the last few years of gradually gaining awareness in the Higher Planes.

A piercing ray of red light traveled across the waves as the sun rose behind dark clouds on the horizon.

"I don't know very much," I said softly.

"You will know your place in the worlds of GOD, and you have indicated what you wanted to do. Do you recall the discourse on the fourteen bands of Self?"

I thought for a moment and realized that I struggled with the mystery for quite a while and then had given the puzzle up entirely.

"You have gained most of the bands of awareness."

I wasn't expecting Him to say that. "Do you mean that?" I asked.

"You have lived the experience instead of putting every glimmer of thought under a microscope, so you have not marked the realizations with a mental image. The bands interrelate with each other, and they build on themselves and provide you with the ability to experience more. The experience is correctly seen as a present realization of all you know, not the marked passage of events, nor a future point to have gained. You are living in the *now*, and when you do this you may not ever see what the world imagines as the process of growth. When you are young on the path you will think in Lower World terms, thus the illustration of the fourteen bands of Self. These levels of awareness are real but they are extremely subtle.

"You will know your position, though the higher in the worlds one goes the more humble one becomes. This will enable you to do the work."

"I don't know that I'm able to carry that load."

The waves seemed to crash louder on the shore as the sun rose over the clouds.

"You are humbled by the experience of approaching IT, we all are. It is not your knowledge of GOD that takes you to ITS presence, it's your lack of attachment. You are aware of Soul and the reason for Its being, and you will continue to gain awareness in the GOD Worlds. Live in this moment in the power of all you are, *right now*. You do not have to carry the world, you only do your work as IT has allowed you to do."

He was right, as always, and I felt blessed in having His guidance and friendship. I turned to thank Him and the rising sun flooded my eyes. When I shaded them to see Him He was gone.

25

Attaining
The Mastership

I heard autumn giving in to winter as the northern wind blew the dried oak leaves across the porch of the studio. Wrapping a quilt tighter around me, I ignored the open windows that would reveal only the darkness of the early morning.

A moment later I stood in Soul awareness, and the Sound seemed to softly glide a few feet from the surface across all of the vast plane of existence before me. The Sound grew louder, though not heard, It was known to every atom that I knew as myself. Every part of me began to ring in a higher note, even the areas that had been forgotten in eternal sleep somewhere in the distant, primal elements of Soul, and recognized the Sound and responded.

For a second I thought of my body left behind in the physical world and I knew I had a choice as to whether I would return to it. Awareness was shifted instantly, and I opened my eyes to view the darkened room of shadows. I felt the breath pass through my lips and the cold of the morning air on my face. The decision was mine; I understood the importance of having the choice, yet there was only one decision I could make for that moment. The body tingled and felt numb from the higher energy of containing the dual awareness. I closed my eyes as the body began to shake in the bed, and I dropped the outer coverings as I traveled higher through the planes.

I rested in an area I had not previously known, though all of it seemed similar to where I had been before. The intensity of the atmosphere, the presence of IT, was greater here. The Sound was subtle, as if It sang in the trees as the wind by a rambling river, It gently caressed the senses of Soul. I could have stayed in that place and would be there now but for the voice I heard in the distance.

My entire being vibrated in the soft Sound, and the persistent voice gradually grew louder. I listened and understood the voice; it sounded like a friend I had not heard from since first leaving this region at some point in my far away memory. The vibration slowly subsided as I listened more intently, and I realized that the voice was the active element of the Self. I had nearly become the Sound, the complete act of *being,* and then, just before blending all awareness in the tonal wave of GOD, I knew to shift my awareness further into the heavens by using the inner power of Soul.

There is no movement in the GOD Worlds, there is but the realization of Self in the ever expanding experience. By becoming the experience itself, or *being,* we become increasingly more aware of IT and all ITS manifestations. Soul can be content to rest within the area It has harmonized with until It wishes to become aware of another part of the GOD Worlds. The attention shifts to a new point, the experience broadens, and the *knowing* process continues.

When my awareness shifted I felt as if I were propelled through a void, and yet there was evidence of a warmth and power all around me. My attention became fixed after some time. The soft, offwhite glow of this new environment seemed to suspend me in a space that would easily hold ten universes of material matter. This is not an exaggeration. I marveled at the vastness and then realized that I did not sense the Sound, but rather there was a silent pulse within me that made me aware of the Sound. I reflected on the visions before me, on the multicolored Light that moved in and around the space as lightning beams of energy and then would slowly diffuse into a golden mist of immense size. The Light had no apparent source, but I sensed that It was formed from a point just beyond the perimeter of this world. I *knew* there was more to understand if I could be closer to the source of the Light.

In a blinding rush of awareness I was suddenly falling at an incredible speed with no immediate control. I was moving faster and faster, but not downward as I at first believed. I was moving outward, as if all of me were accelerating three hundred and sixty degrees outward from the core of my *being*. A whirring sound eased into my consciousness, growing louder as I traveled further without direction. The atmosphere changed from a golden mist to a veil of an orange hue and then into the most intense white Light that I had ever known.

The Light burned into my Self, It stripped me of the momentary awareness of myself, while the Sound filled me with the low, rhythmic pulse of what I *knew* was the Source. I accepted the Light and I absorbed the Sound, so much that I became the Sound and the Light, all at once, and was swept into the Power of It. I was part of the nature of Spirit, which is next to the very heart of GOD.

And then there was darkness, silence, and no movement anywhere in my awareness.

In my awareness I *knew*, "I am this," but I was more than that realization. I was part of a much more inclusive and embracing knowledge, though I *knew* the knowledge was not me, I was a fragment of IT. I could not sense my Soul awareness, nor could I see or hear the presence of Spirit, there was but the total realm of *being* present, and I understood my place in this *being*.

At some point later I could sense the far away roar as I witnessed the Light roll over Itself in marvelous images. The Light then danced in the pulse of the Voice that spoke within me. IT was the Voice of Love, of Power, of ALL. I marveled at the representation of GOD, and I *knew* the Voice was but the image of the silence and the Power of IT ITSELF.

I awoke staring out the open window. My mind was blank, my emotions were dead calm, and my body was numb. Gradually I was able to move to the end of the bed and I rolled onto the floor. I laid there for some time, and I couldn't understand why I *knew* what I knew, though I had no thoughts of what I *knew,* but I did *know* more than I could ever bring back into that room and into this world.

The rain fell lightly across the city as I later sat in front of the glass door and drank a cup of mint tea. The light of the day grew dim, and it was then that I realized that the sun was setting behind the wall of dark clouds.

I sat at the desk for hours, still unable to formulate my senses into images or thoughts. Around midnight I forced myself to walk outside, and then as the rain chilled my body I slowly returned to this world. I walked on in the night, past the apartments of subdued light, the buildings empty of business, and at last to the railroad tracks. Sitting on the rail I wondered if I had experienced what I sensed, not knowing exactly what I thought IT was, but *knowing* IT was profound.

I came to no mental conclusions that night, nor the next day. I decided to live the experience as best I could.

In trying today to describe these events I know that I could fill volumes with the sensory images of what I experienced, but really there is nothing I can possibly say that will begin to share with you the magnitude and intensity of those worlds. Words and thoughts are, at best, very crude representations of what the mind can only imagine to be the Worlds of GOD. The Reality of IT is to be experienced.

Several weeks went by without a remarkable experience, and I was thankful for the rest. I felt a little more distant, and it was somewhat harder to keep my attention on my job. I had a lot of work to do, I knew that, but I did not know precisely what it was that I was to do. Four months before I had released a new book of poems, *Secrets,* and had been placing it in stores across the Southeast. That project was important, but it was not the primary responsibility I felt. My conscious mind could not hold the thought of where I was going. It was much like knowing that there is something important that you need to do, but you can't recall just what it is. I sensed that my decision had been reached, and I knew that I would bridge the information through to my consciousness in due time.

I was feeling very tired one afternoon and came home at a

reasonable hour for a change, to fall immediately into bed. The second I laid down I was wide awake and rested. Knowing my body needed the rest I imagined I was tired and proceeded to gradually fall asleep.

I became aware of being in a valley, though not the training ground near Shantok. This area seemed to be in a higher elevation, with more jagged peaks and ridges covered in snow. Dried grass leaned southward from the wind that swept through the massive stone walls, and fine particles of ice seemed to be suspended in the air.

I heard what sounded like a melody played on a flute, though it could have been the wind against the rocks. I started walking toward the sound and saw a narrow, worn path that was almost hidden behind brush. As I approached the path I sensed danger and stopped. I could not detect the threat so I ventured on. I walked for almost an hour as the path led me around the outer edges of the mountain. There was no sign of life anywhere.

At one point I rested on a boulder that hung over the edge, and I enjoyed the spectacular view of the hazy mountain ranges. It occurred to me all of once what I had been trying so hard to remember. I had bridged the information with part of my mind, and I had an image of what work I had chosen to do on this planet. I accepted the responsibility within myself, it had been my decision, after all. I spent a while on the boulder reflecting on the beauty and the magnitude of the view and on my own challenges that lay ahead.

I heard conversation coming from far off, perhaps above me somewhere on the mountain. I started on the path again and eventually saw a group of people standing together in a clearing. I recognized a few of the people as having worked with me on the inner planes.

Suddenly the overwhelming image of the master who had been banished from the Order stood in front of me, blocking me from joining the group. His presence was very powerful and grew in intensity, so much that I could feel pressure on every square inch of my body. I lifted my hands instinctively, with palms outward, and focused most of my energy through

my palms, piercing the image of the once respected master.
The intense blue current of power that came from me caused
the image to spark, and the electric bolts arced across the
outer ridge of the form of the master. His face grew larger
and then there was a loud rumble that seemed to shake the
rock I was standing on. The image broke up into a smokey
mist of atoms, and after a few seconds I could see the group
of Masters watching me across the way.

I realized that I had been confronted by an image, a mock
up, and not the actual form of the master. I sensed that it was
an attack, however, by that master, and not a test provided
by the Order. I had worked briefly with that master when he
carried the responsibility of being the *One* who channels
Spirit, but had long severed my ties with him.

I approached the Order and several Masters started
laughing, then they shook my hand. Paul slapped me on the
back and said, "You don't do anything in a small way, do
you? That's the determination it takes to do this work, and
now you have entered into it firsthand."

I looked into His eyes and saw all of time reflected there.
I shook His hand and could say nothing. When I turned I
saw Ramini standing off to one side. He was smiling. He and
Paul and I walked together for a while with several of the
others, and they talked about various adventures each of
them had been part of.

I awoke in my physical body late into the night, and I immediately remembered what had happened. Sitting on the
side of the bed I wondered for a moment if I had imagined all
of it. My inner voice, the voice beyond the mind, spoke clearly in Soul awareness, saying, "Only I know the truth of my
life, no one else can tell me where I have been." I laughed
softly to myself and moved toward the bookcase on sudden
impulse and started to pick up *The Tiger's Fang*, by Paul
Twitchell. As my hand touched the cover I could see a blue
electric pulse of energy pass from my fingers to the book. I
stopped suddenly, and then picked the book up as the energy
subsided. As I thumbed through the pages, remembering
that this was the book Hutch had given me years before, I immediately recognized and knew the vibratory pattern of His

written words. They carried a sense and reality of the GOD Worlds that I had experienced, though I did not recognize many of the physical descriptions of His experiences. I knew the difference was in the experience and in His description of the mental concepts.

I sat in the chair beside the desk, reached up to turn off the lamp, and heard the two thirty-three rumble down the tracks, and then whistle loudly at the crossing by the college. A baby was crying somewhere in an apartment down the way and then hushed upon being held. These sounds brought me momentarily back to life in the material world, and I realized that I enjoyed being part of this time and place on the planet.

I sensed the presence of Paul, and turned to see Him sitting in the other chair. I remarked to Him that I felt so inadequate to write about my discoveries. I asked Him, "How can I write about what you have shown me? Words seem so useless to describe the reality of what I realize."

It was then that He reminded me of how we use words as images of the eternal Sound, and though it was difficult, if not impossible, to bring the Higher World realizations into print, our words were some of the instruments used to guide those who are ready into the GOD Worlds. I have quoted Him explaining this in the first chapter of this book.

He then went on to talk about balancing the forces within.

"Your work will keep you in the public consciousness, though you will work unknown to most people. I know that you sit here late into the night to collect your thoughts and gather your energy after working in the world all day. I used to walk the beach at night, when possible. Sometimes the late night streets of the city were the only peace I could find in a day.

"Never has the planet had so much information at its fingertips; never has it seen the level of stress and confusion that it faces now. All this information may appear to answer the spiritual questions and uplift people, but in fact it bogs them down. Part of the work involves sifting the words and concepts down into the truth of Soul.

"You can live in the wilderness and avoid the frenzied activity, except that you work with many on the inner awareness, and they carry their frustrations with them, even on the inner planes. You will learn to use your time wisely, we have so little time for so much work here.

"As you become used to carrying the work you will learn to *be* in the action of it. When you carry the thoughts and the emotions of what the work appears to be you will be exhausted by the load. Simply *be* all that you are, each second, and do what you must do. You are a law unto yourself, you cannot be wrong, you are IT, and IT is within you. The difference is subtle, indeed, being only the element of Self. *Act, be,* and work within the Love and Power of IT, and IT will provide the rest."

I sat in the dark in silence, amazed and humbled by all that had happened.

26
Now

I lived in the studio for another ten months, and then I married a woman I had met shortly after the last visit I described with Paul. I was shown the opportunity to meet her on the inner planes and saw the potential for much spiritual sharing. I followed up on that information. But that is another story, for another time.

Debbi and I now live outside of Atlanta, and we've seen many changes over the four years since leaving the studio. We both have fond memories of that place, and she shared the warmth and the energy that surrounded that time.

Our careers have shifted dramatically, and there have been many challenges. Each situation has led to a better understanding of our lives, and we have been provided with more than what we could have anticipated.

What I've expressed in this book are the highlights of my experience. It is important to remember that I lived each moment, each hour, each day, and each year as best I could realize life at that time. While realization is often a slow process, it is sometimes blinding in its intensity.

I have studied many metaphysical teachings first hand, both in this life and in past lives. I have researched the oral and written accounts of hundreds of people who have found a reality apart from the one most people accept. I have learned that there is no one reality that most people accept, there is but the personal experience, and that must be proven by each person.

The most basic spiritual principles were outlined to me on the inner planes by several different Masters, and while some of the teachings differed in expression and format from Paul's written teachings, the essence was the same.

What I have known is not unique, yet you may not find what I have found. We are each so different in our awareness, and even though all paths eventually take us to our true home, the view on the journey depends on the method and route of travel, as well as the ability to see what is before you.

It was many years after making contact with Ramini before I understood that there was so much more beyond metaphysics. He told me of the GOD Worlds, and He pointed out the limitations of many of the studies I was involved in, but I did not make the connection for a long time. I thought I understood, but I was mistaken. He provided me with the information, and much later I came to *know* what He meant as my awareness broadened. It was very much a step-by-step process of realization, one that spanned years in this life; and in truth, was many, many lifetimes in the making. In this aspect, my journey is much like everyone else's. So often we can lose patience with the process and want GOD realization right this minute. If we were allowed that experience before we had conditioned our Lower World bodies we would literally burn them to a crisp.

Our pattern of growth is an individual course, and each of us raises the vibratory rate in varying degrees, over varying periods of time. The realizations can be so subtle that you may not appreciate the progess you've made. The goal is not to have the experiences, but to realize the spiritual lessons the experiences may provide. Often you may realize the lessons without the conscious, profound experience, and you may feel that you are not growing like someone whose life is full of inner plane adventures. When you look at your life from this perspective you are looking for the phenomena of the spiritual worlds, not the spiritual realizations.

I can tell you that everyone will gain realization of their

true Self, Soul, just as everyone will know GOD, in their own pace and time. This is the promise of Soul. Most people do not desire these experiences in their present states of awareness. It serves no purpose to try to persuade these people that they should desire GOD. Each Soul will seek GOD when It is ready, and if It wants GOD enough, then nothing can stand in the way. Each Soul is growing perfectly in place within the play of life, no matter the state of awareness.

From time to time I am asked if I can prove the events in my life or my awareness. I don't know how to prove my life to someone else, but I can tell you that I prove each experience to myself before I accept it. Knowledge cannot be taught or given, it must be "caught," as Paul is fond of saying. Each person has to prove their existence to themselves by their own personal standard of belief and understanding. Perhaps the accounts of my life can serve as a measure of some realizations, a gauge to judge the process of growing beyond conventional thought and understanding.

The reality is in the living, not in the mental comprehension or in the emotional feelings of oneness with this world. The proof is in living life each moment to your fullest aspect of *knowing*. You can live the experience that is truly yours, that is determined by your proof, in your awareness. Once you begin to approach life from this viewpoint, the opinions and thoughts of others will mean less and less, and your search for the inner truth in life will expand to fulfill you beyond belief. It doesn't matter what someone else tells you about yourself; it matters only what you *know* to be true.

The role of the Master is to suggest a course to follow in the spiritual realms and to assist you in *knowing* your true Self, and GOD. If you are not working directly with a Master you may ask Spirit to provide what is best in your life, best for your awareness at this time. The Master approaches you only by your request.

In my view the world has enough religions, philosophies, cults, studies, and countless followings. There is a time and place for group sharing of concepts with others, and this can be helpful when one first starts on the path. However, one does not find GOD as part of a group effort or by realizing a concept.

It has never been my intention to create yet another following for the human consciousness to involve itself in. I have chosen not to use or assign a name to this body of higher information, though many names have been used over time. In my experience, GOD IS. All the rest is an attempt to find thoughts, concepts, words, and systems to explain that fact.

We are alone in our seach for GOD, aided for a time by the Master. The spiritual information in this book is older than time itself, older than all the Lower Worlds, and does not belong to one group or study, or to one man. Your proof will be personal and will be discovered alone as you make your way on the spiritual path. This is really the only way it can be.

You and I have shared a brief time together here. Perhaps we will meet again.

Eliott James lives near Atlanta, Georgia. He is currently working on two new book projects as well as lecturing and presenting Soul Awareness workshops across the country.

If you would like more information about the material discussed in this book, please feel free to write the author in care of the publisher:

Dhamma Books
Post Office Box 724947
Atlanta, Georgia 30339